Scotland History

Early History, The People, Culture and Tradition

Author
Idris Mills

Copyright Notice

Copyright © 2017 Global Print Digital
All Rights Reserved

Digital Management Copyright Notice. This Title is not in public domain, it is copyrighted to the original author, and being published by **Global Print Digital**. No other means of reproducing this title is accepted, and none of its content is editable, neither right to commercialize it is accepted, except with the consent of the author or authorized distributor. You must purchase this Title from a vendor who's right is given to sell it, other sources of purchase are not accepted, and accountable for an action against. We are happy that you understood, and being guided by these terms as you proceed. Thank you

First Printing: 2017.

ISBN: 978-1-912483-13-6

Publisher: Global Print Digital.
Arlington Row, Bibury, Cirencester GL7 5ND
Gloucester
United Kingdom.
Website: www.homeworkoffer.com

Table of Content

Introduction 1
Land 5
    Relief 6
    Drainage 10
    Soils 11
    Climate 12
    Plant and animal life 13
People 17
    Ethnic groups 19
    Languages 20
    Settlement patterns 22
    Demographic trends 25
    Gender Roles and Statuses 26
    Marriage, Family, and Kinship 28
    Secular Celebrations 31
Economy 34
    Agriculture, forestry, and fishing 35
    Forestry 38
    Fishing 39
    Resources and power 40
    Manufacturing 42
    Finance 45
    Services 47
    Transportation 48
Government and Society 52
    Constitutional framework 52
    Local government 54
    Justice 55
    Political process 57
    Security 60
    Health and welfare 61
    Housing 62
    Education 63

Cultural and Tradition 69
Highland/Gaelic Culture 70
Highland Games 72
Highland Dress 74
Bagpipes 74
Food and Drink 76
Ceilidh 78
Religion 78
Sports and recreation 79
Daily life and social customs 83
The arts 86
Cultural institutions 97
Media and publishing 98
History 101
Ancient times 101
The unification of the kingdom 113
The development of the monarchy 117
David I (1124–53) 119
Medieval economy and society 122
The Wars of Independence 128
Scotland in the 15th century 136
15th-century society 144
Scotland in the 16th and early 17th centuries 149
Mary (1542–67) and the Scottish Reformation 152
The Age of Revolution (1625–89) 164
The Restoration monarchy 170
The era of union 172
19th-century Scotland 182
The Industrial Revolution 184
Politics and religion 187
The Highlands 189
Scotland since World War I 191
World War II and after 194
The establishment of a Scottish Parliament 202

Introduction

Scotland is the most northerly of the four parts of the United Kingdom, occupying about one-third of the island of Great Britain. The name Scotland derives from the Latin Scotia, land of the Scots, a Celtic people from Ireland who settled on the west coast of Great Britain about the 5th century ad. The name Caledonia has often been applied to Scotland, especially in poetry. It is derived from Caledonii, the Roman name of a tribe in the northern part of what is now Scotland.

An austere land, subject to extremes of weather, Scotland has proved a difficult home for countless generations of its people, who have nonetheless prized it for its beauty and unique culture. "I am a Scotsman," the poet and novelist Sir Walter Scott wrote in the 19th century; "therefore I had to fight my way into the world." Historically one of Europe's poorest countries, Scotland has contributed much to political and practical theories of progress: forged in the Scottish Enlightenment in the hands of such philosophers as Francis Hutcheson, Adam Smith, and David Hume, who viewed humankind as a product of history and the "pursuit of happiness" as an inalienable right, this progressive ideal contributed substantially to the development of modern democracy.

Scots have also played a vital role in many of the world's most important scientific and technological innovations, with inventors, engineers, and entrepreneurs such as Alexander Graham Bell, James Watt, Andrew Carnegie, and John McAdam extending Scotland's reach far beyond the small country's borders. Few students of English-language literature are unacquainted with historian Thomas Carlyle, poet Robert Burns, and novelist Muriel Spark.

Scotland's relations with England, with which it was merged in 1707 to form the United Kingdom of Great Britain, have long been difficult. Although profoundly influenced by the English, Scotland has long refused to consider itself as anything other than a separate country, and it has bound itself to historical fact and legend alike in an effort to retain national identity, as well as to the distinct dialect of English called Scots; writing defiantly of his country's status, the nationalist poet Hugh MacDiarmid proclaimed: "For we ha'e faith in Scotland's hidden poo'ers, The present's theirs, but a' the past and future's oors." That independent spirit bore fruit in 1996, when the highly symbolic Stone of Scone was returned to Edinburgh, Scotland's capital, from London, and in 1999 a new Scottish Parliament the first since 1707 was elected and given significant powers over Scottish affairs.

Edinburgh is a handsome city of great historical significance and one of Europe's chief cultural centres. Other significant principal cities include Glasgow, Dundee, Aberdeen, and Perth, all centres for industry, transportation, and commerce.

Hardworking, practical, and proud of their traditions, the Scots have a reputation for thrift that verges on miserliness. Travelers to the country, however, often remark on the generosity and friendliness of their hosts, as well as on the vibrancy of contemporary Scottish culture. An ancient Gaelic song, a blessing on cattle and the people who keep them, speaks to that hospitality in a sometimes inhospitable landscape:

Land

Scotland is bounded by England to the south, the Atlantic Ocean to the west and north, and the North Sea to the east. The west coast is fringed by deep indentations (sea lochs or fjords) and by numerous islands, varying in size from mere rocks to the large landmasses of Lewis and Harris, Skye, and Mull. The island clusters of Orkney and Shetland lie to the north. At its greatest length, measured from Cape Wrath to the Mull of Galloway, the mainland of Scotland extends 274 miles (441 km), while the maximum breadth measured from Applecross, in the western Highlands, to Buchan Ness, in the eastern Grampian Mountains is

154 miles (248 km). But, because of the deep penetration of the sea in the sea lochs and firths (estuaries), most places are within 40 to 50 miles (65 to 80 km) of the sea, and only 30 miles (50 km) of land separate the Firth of Clyde and the Firth of Forth, the two great estuarine inlets on the west and east coasts, respectively.

Relief

Scotland is traditionally divided into three topographic areas: the Highlands in the north, the Midland Valley (Central Lowlands), and the Southern Uplands. (The latter two areas are included in the Lowlands cultural region.) Low-lying areas extend through the Midland Valley and along the greater part of the eastern seaboard. The east coast contrasts with the west in its smoother outline and thus creates an east-west distinction in topography as well as a north-south one. The Highlands are bisected by the fault line of Glen

Mor (Glen Albyn), which is occupied by a series of lochs (lakes), the largest of which is Loch Ness, famous for its probably mythical monster. North of Glen Mor is an ancient plateau, which, through long erosion, has been cut into a series of peaks of fairly uniform height separated by glens (valleys) carved out by glaciers. The northwestern fringe of the mainland is particularly barren, the rocks of the Lewisian Complex having been worn down by severe glaciation to produce a hummocky landscape, dotted by small lochs and rocks protruding from thin, acidic soil. The landscape is varied by spectacular Torridonian sandstone mountains, weathered into sheer cliffs, rock terraces, and pinnacles.

Southeast of Glen Mor are the Grampian Mountains (also shaped by glaciation), though there are intrusions such as the granitic masses of the Cairngorm Mountains. The Grampians are on the whole less rocky and rugged than the mountains of the northwest, being more rounded and grassy with wider plateau areas. But many have cliffs and pinnacles that provide challenges for mountaineers, and the area contains Britain's highest mountains, reaching a maximum elevation of 4,406 feet (1,343 metres) at Ben Nevis. There are some flatter areas the most striking being Rannoch Moor, a bleak expanse of bogs and granitic rocks with narrow, deep lochs such as Rannoch and Ericht. The southeastern margin of the Highlands is clearly marked by the Highland Boundary Fault, running northeast to southwest from Stonehaven, just south of Aberdeen, to Helensburgh on the River Clyde and passing through Loch Lomond, Scotland's largest stretch of inland water.

The southern boundary of the Midland Valley is not such a continuous escarpment, but the fault beginning in the northeast with the Lammermuir and Moorfoot hills and extending to Glen App, in the southwest, is a distinct dividing line. In some ways the label Lowlands is a misnomer, for, although this part of Scotland is low by comparison with adjoining areas, it is by no means flat. The landscape includes hills such as the Sidlaws, the Ochils, the Campsies, and the Pentlands, composed of volcanic rocks rising as high as 1,898 feet (579 metres). The Southern Uplands are not as high as the Highlands.

Glaciation has produced narrow, flat valleys separating rolling mountains. To the east of Nithsdale the hills are rounded, gently sloping, and grass-covered, providing excellent grazing for sheep, and they open out along the valley of the lower Tweed into the rich farming land of the Merse. To the west of Nithsdale the landscape is rougher, with granitic intrusions around Loch Doon, and the soil is more peaty and wet. The high moorlands and hills, reaching up to 2,766 feet (843 metres) at Merrick, are also suitable for sheep farming. The uplands slope toward the coastal plains along the Solway Firth in the south and to the machair and the Mull of Galloway farther west.

Drainage

Uplift and an eastward tilting of the Highlands some 50 million years ago (during the Eocene Epoch) formed a watershed near the west coast. As a result, most rivers drain eastward, but deeply glaciated rock basins in the northern Highlands form numerous large lochs. There are fewer lochs in the Grampian Mountains, although the area contains the large lochs of Ericht, Rannoch, and Tay. Well-graded rivers such as the Dee, the Don, and the Spey meander eastward and northeastward to the North Sea. The Tay and Forth emerge from the southern Grampians to flow out of the eastern Lowlands in two large estuaries. The Clyde and the Tweed both rise in the Southern Uplands, the one flowing west into the Firth of Clyde and the other east into the North Sea, while the Nith, the Annan, and a few other rivers run south into the Solway Firth. Lochs are numerous in the Highlands, ranging from moraine-dammed lochans (pools) in mountain corries (cirques) to large and deep lochs filling rock basins. In the Lowlands and the Southern Uplands, lochs are shallower and less numerous.

Soils

With Scotland's diversity in geologic structure, relief, and weather, the character of the soil varies greatly. In the northwest, the Hebrides, the Shetland Islands, and other areas, the soil is poor and rocky, and cultivation is possible only at river mouths, glens, and coastal strips. On the west coast of some Hebridean islands, however, there are stretches of calcareous sand (the machair) suitable for farming. Peat is widespread on moors and hills. Areas with good, arable land have largely been derived from old red sandstone and younger rocks, as in the Orkney Islands, the eastern

Highlands, the northeastern coastal plain, and the Lowlands.

Climate

Scotland has a temperate oceanic climate, milder than might be expected from its latitude. Despite its small area, there are considerable variations. Precipitation is greatest in the mountainous areas of the west, as prevailing winds, laden with moisture from the Atlantic, blow from the southwest. East winds are common in winter and spring, when cold, dry continental air masses envelop the east coast. Hence, the west tends to be milder in winter, with less frost and with snow seldom lying long at lower elevations, but it is damper and cloudier than the east in summer. Tiree, in the Inner Hebrides off the west coast, has a mean temperature in winter of 41 °F (5 °C) in the coldest month (as high as southeastern England), whereas Dundee, on the east coast, has 37 °F (3 °C).

Dundee's mean temperature in the warmest month is 59 °F (15 °C) and Tiree's 57 °F (14 °C). There is a smaller range of temperatures over the year in Scotland than in southern England. Precipitation varies remarkably. Some two-thirds of Scotland receives more than 40 inches (1,000 mm) annually, the average for Britain, with the total reaching 142 inches (3,600 mm) in the Ben Nevis area and somewhat more near Loch Quoich farther to the northwest. In the flat Outer Hebrides conditions are less humid, as in the east, where the Moray Firth receives annually less than 25 inches (635 mm) and Dundee less than 32 inches (810 mm). A significant amount of snow falls above 1,500 feet (460 metres) in the Highlands in winter.

Plant and animal life

Lower elevations, up to about 1,500 feet, were once covered with natural forests, which have been cleared over the course of centuries and replaced in some areas by trees, plants, and crops. Survivals of the original forest are found sporadically throughout the Highlands for example, in the pinewoods of Rothiemurchus in the Spey valley. Grass and heather cover most of the Grampians and the Southern Uplands, where the soil is not so wet and dank as in the northwestern Highlands. Shrubs such as bearberry, crowberry, and blaeberry (bilberry) grow on peaty soil, as does bog cotton. Alpine and Arctic species flourish on the highest slopes and plateaus of the Grampians, including saxifrages, creeping azalea, and dwarf willows. Ben Lawers is noted for its plentiful mountain flora.

Scotland is rich in animal life for its size. Herds of red deer graze in the corries and remote glens; although formerly woodland dwellers, they are now found mainly on higher ground, but roe deer still inhabit the woods, along with sika and fallow deer (both introduced species) in some areas. Foxes and badgers are widespread, but the Scottish wildcat has become critically endangered as a result of disease and interbreeding with domestic cats. Rabbits were once decimated by the disease myxomatosis but have largely recovered to earlier numbers. Pine marten, otters, and mountain and brown hares are among other wild mammals. A few ospreys nest in Scotland, and golden eagles, buzzards, peregrine falcons, and kestrels are the most notable of resident birds of prey. The red grouse, the Scottish subspecies of the willow grouse, has long been hunted for sport. Other species of grouse include the ptarmigan, found only at higher elevations, and the large capercaillie, which has been reintroduced into Scotland's pine woodlands. Large numbers of seabirds, such as gannets, fulmars, guillemots, and gulls, breed on cliffs and on the stacks (isolated rocks) around the magnificent coasts. More than one-third of the world's Atlantic, or gray, seals breed in Scottish waters, especially around the

Northern and Western Isles, as do numerous common seals; dolphins and porpoises are regularly seen and whales occasionally, especially on the west coast.

People

Warm, fun-loving and generous Scottish people

Scottish people have a worldwide reputation for warmth and friendliness. Whether it's the millions of visitors who travel to Scotland every year or the thousands who come to live permanently, so many talk of a genuine friendliness and a welcoming hospitality.

Did you know that almost three quarters of European visitors say that one of the main reasons for visiting Scotland is its people?

Everyday friendliness

The Scots love people and they like to make others feel at home. You'll find an enthusiastic friendliness in so many places. Ask a stranger for directions, buy something in a local shop, eat or drink in a pub or restaurant or put on the kettle in your workplace kitchen and you'll be met with a smiling face and a friendly "Let me help", "Tell me more about yourself" or "How are you?"

Culture and identity
Scottish people are proud of their nationality but they also have a long tradition of welcoming new people and cultures. Historically, Scotland has appreciated the benefits of embracing different cultures.

Today, Scotland is a richly diverse country with dozens of different cultures living in harmony. Tolerance, equality of opportunity and social justice are important principles of Scottish people and communities.

We love a party

Scotland knows how to party and extends an invitation to all. From large Hogmanay (New Year's Eve) street parties and music and film festivals to more intimate Burns' Suppers and St Andrew's Day celebrations, there is always a fun event to attend.

Getting together, sharing good times, 'having a blether' and welcoming others with open arms give Scotland its reputation for being a happy and friendly country.

Really, it's no wonder that 50 million people around the world claim Scottish ancestry and so many want to be a part of our Scottish family.

In this section, you'll find all the facts about Scotland you need to know, including information about the Scottish population, their language as well as famous Scottish people.

Ethnic groups

For many centuries continual strife characterized relations between the Celtic Scots of the Highlands and the western islands and the Anglo-Saxons of the Lowlands. Only since the 20th century has the mixture been widely seen as a basis for a rich unified Scottish culture; the people of Shetland and Orkney have tended to remain apart from both of these elements and to look to Scandinavia as the mirror of their Norse heritage. Important immigrant groups have arrived, most notably Irish labourers; there have also been significant groups of Jews, Lithuanians, Italians, and, after World War II, Poles and others, as well as a more recent influx of Asians, especially from Pakistan. The enlargement of the European Union in 2004 led to a dramatic increase in immigration from the countries of eastern Europe.

Languages

Scotland's linguistic heritage is complex. The vast majority of the population now speaks English, but both Scottish Gaelic and the Scots language have wide influence. Languages such as Urdu and Punjabi continue to be spoken by immigrant groups, and the Scottish Parliament provides information in different languages to meet these needs.

Gaelic, the Celtic language brought from Ireland by the Scots, is spoken by only a tiny proportion of the Scottish population, mainly concentrated in the Western Isles and the western Highlands, with pockets elsewhere, especially in Glasgow. Interest in Gaelic has increased sharply, especially following the establishment of the new Scottish Parliament in 1999, and its literature has flourished. Scots was originally a form of Old English that diverged from southern forms of the language in the Middle Ages, becoming a separate national tongue by the 15th century.

Union with England and other factors caused English gradually to be adopted as the official and standard language; however, Scots survives in the Lowland areas, in a vigorous tradition of poetry and drama, and in aspects of the English spoken by most Scots. Both Gaelic and Scots are recorded and supported by major works of scholarship: the Linguistic Survey of Scotland (1975–86), The Scottish National Dictionary (1931–75), and A Dictionary of the Older Scottish Tongue (1931–2002). The Scottish government has allocated funds to support Gaelic, notably in broadcasting and education, and it also has provided grants to Scots-language organizations. Local education authorities are required to provide for the teaching of Gaelic in Gaelic-speaking areas, and they give guidance on ways to include Scots literature in school curricula.

Settlement patterns

In earlier times mountains, rivers, and seas divided the Scottish people into self-sufficient communities that developed strong senses of local identity. This sense has been eroded by social mobility, modern transport, broadcasting, and other standardizing influences and by a general shift from rural to urban ways of life. Yet vestiges of regional consciousness linger. The Shetland islanders speak of Scotland with detachment. The Galloway area in the southwest, cut off by hills from the rest of the country, has a vigorous regional patriotism. The Gaelic-speaking people of the Hebrides and the western Highlands find their language a bond of community. The northeast has its own local traditions, embodied especially in a still vigorous Scots dialect, and Borderers celebrate their local festivals with fervour. The most thickly populated rural areas are those with the best farming land, such as in East Lothian and in the northeast.

The Highlands once nourished a large population, but "Highland Clearances" (a series of forcible evictions) and continuous emigration since the 18th century have caused it to dwindle. Now settlements in the Highlands are mostly remnants of crofting townships that is, irregular groupings of subsistence farms of a few acres each. The old pattern of crofting was one of communities practicing a kind of cooperative farming, with strips of common land allotted annually to individuals. Examples of the old system survive, but now crofters have their own arable land fenced in, while they share the common grazing land. In East Lothian and other areas of high farming, the communal farm has long been replaced by single farms with steadings (farmsteads) and workers' houses. Scotland noticeably lacks those old villages that evolved in England from medieval hamlets of joint tenants. Some planned villages were built by enterprising landowners in the 18th century.

Burghs, often little bigger than villages, were mostly set up as trading centres, ports, or river crossings or to command entrances to mountain passes. Many small towns survive around the east and northeast coast that were once obliged to be self-contained in consumer industries and burghal institutions because they lacked adequate transportation systems. The growth of industry and transport has helped produce urbanization. Edinburgh, Dundee, and Aberdeen are centres of administration, commerce, and industry for their areas, but only central Clydeside, including Glasgow with its satellite towns, is large enough to deserve the official title of conurbation (metropolitan area).

Demographic trends

While Scotland makes up about one-third of the area of the United Kingdom, it has less than one-tenth of the population, of which the greatest concentration (nearly three-fourths) lives in the central belt. Historically, England has been the main beneficiary of Scottish emigration, especially during economic downturns. Large-scale emigration also placed Scots in such countries as Canada, the United States, and Australia until the late 20th century; despite this phenomenon, however, the size of the Scottish population has remained relatively stable since World War II. The pattern of migration began to reverse when the North Sea petroleum industry brought many people to the northeast and the north, not only from various parts of Scotland and the United Kingdom but also from other countries, notably the United States. Scotland is now increasingly seen as an attractive place to work and live.

Gender Roles and Statuses

Division of Labor by Gender. Women are beginning to outstrip men as a percentage of total employees.

Scottish machismo, bolstered by laborism, Calvinism, militarism, and soccer is adjusting to a

world where the association of women with domesticity and reproduction and men with public life and paid employment are weakening. However, life chances are far from equal. Men far outnumber women in elected political offices, the legal profession, and managerial and administrative positions in business. Women earn 72 percent of what men earn on average, and are concentrated in certain economic sectors (shops, hotels, financial and business services, education, health, and social work) and the voluntary sector. Subject choices by sex in education suggest that gendered work expectations endure, with construction, engineering, manufacture and production, and transport being over-whelming male and personal care, office and secretarial, and social work overwhelmingly female.

The Relative Status of Women and Men. Men and women are notionally equal, but there is still room for reform. The feminist movement has opposed sex discrimination, fought to ensure greater participation by women in the new parliament, and had some success heightening awareness about violence against women. Still, many young men and women consider it acceptable to hit a woman or force her to have sex in certain circumstances. Women, especially as single parents and pensioners, are more vulnerable to poverty than men are, and the vast majority of single parents with dependent children are women.

Marriage, Family, and Kinship

Marriage. Over a third of marriages are civil rather than religious. Scots law requires that marriages be monogamous and be between consenting adults (over age 16) and provides for the recognition of marriage "by habit and repute."

Traditional weddings take place on Friday or Saturday, with the groom in formal attire (often kilted) and the bride usually in white, forbidden to see the groom until the ceremony. Weddings normally are conducted near the bride's home. The bride enters last and is "given away" by her father or a senior male relative. Divorce can be obtained on the bases of adultery, intolerable behavior, desertion, and de facto separation.

Domestic Unit. An increasing number of households (around 30 percent) contain a single adult, while those with one male and one female with children (around 20 percent) have been decreasing. Around a quarter include one male, one female, and no children, and just over 10 percent include three or more adults with no children. At least a third of households are headed by women, a fifth of those widowed or divorced, whereas two thirds of households are headed by men, over half of which are married.

Inheritance. Until the 1960s, the incomes, savings, and properties of both spouses were considered totally separate, with marriage conferring no claims. Parliamentary acts in 1964 and 1985 established equal claims at divorce on most property acquired during marriage, and household goods and savings from housekeeping allowances are equally shared. A peculiarity of Scots law is that minors can enter into binding contracts.

Kin Groups. The clan system today has significance primarily for historians and tourists. Ties of kinship are activated by conditions of class and economic opportunity, with poverty, family businesses, and extreme wealth tending to heighten the importance of kin group obligations. Scotland is a small country with a high degree of overlap in social and kinship networks. Thus, urban networks involving politics and public life can be very dense, creating a sense of familiarity across a wide social field.

Secular Celebrations

Christmas was hardly observed in the Lowlands after the Reformation but is broadly observed as a relatively secularized holiday. New Year's Eve, called Hogmanay, has long been the main midwinter celebration. Fairlike events and public gatherings for the changing of the year are promoted by major cities. Customarily, some entertained guests at home, while others went "firstfooting." First-footers carry a bottle of whiskey and perhaps some food and, if traditional, a lump of coal or something black.

Celtic seasonal rituals fused to medieval saints' days survive in modern secularized celebrations. Traditionally, Halloween (31 October) involved children "guising," or dressing up in costumes and entertaining for treats, engaging in mischief, and young girls performing divination to find out about their future spouses. The May Day celebration of Beltane, involving bonfires on hilltops, has seen a revival. Many towns have fairs and gala weeks, especially during the summer. Annual Highland Gatherings serve a similar civic function, as do the Common Ridings in the Borders towns, in which a horseback procession "beats out" the boundaries of the medieval burgh.

Saint Andrew's Day (30 November), named after the national patron saint, is not marked ritually, but events of national significance are often timed to fall on that day. Perhaps the most symbol-laden holiday is Burns Day (25 January), named after the "national" poet, Robert Burns. Set around a ritual "peasant" meal of haggis (a mixture of oats, offal, and seasonings boiled inside the lining of a sheep's stomach), neeps (turnips), and tatties (potatoes), accompanied by whiskey, the event involves an elaborate series of speeches and set readings from Burns's opus. This ceremony plays upon Burns's bawdy celebration of the common people and penchant for deflating the self-righteous and highborn.

Traditionally very male-dominated and chauvanistic affairs, gender participation is now more equal, and even feminist readings of Burns's radicalism can be found

Economy

During the 1970s and '80s Scotland's economy shared in acute form the problems besetting many European countries, brought about by rapid changes that included the widespread failure of heavy industries. Unemployment became a serious problem, especially in those areas where major industries had declined. Successive governments made efforts to improve these conditions by a variety of measures. Beginning in the 1980s, Scotland's economy benefited from the exploitation of North Sea petroleum and natural gas and from the development of high-technology and other economic sectors.

Scotland remains a small but open economy and accounts for about 5 percent of the United Kingdom's export revenue. Its gross domestic product (GDP) per capita is higher than in all other areas of the United Kingdom outside London and England's eastern regions, and its level of unemployment is fairly low. However, wealth in Scotland is not evenly distributed, and the average unemployment rate hides pockets of much higher unemployment in some regions and localities. Although the British government controls Scotland's macroeconomic policy, including central government spending, interest rates, and monetary matters, the Scottish Parliament has power over local economic development, education, and training.

Agriculture, forestry, and fishing

Wild animals, birds, and river fishes are of minor importance as an economic resource, but deer and grouse hunting, as well as fishing, provides employment in parts of the Highlands in which other activities are hardly possible. Venison, including meat from deer farms, is exported to the European mainland.

Agriculture

No economic sector made greater progress in the post-World War II period than agriculture in terms of productivity. Mechanization allowed the full-time labour force to fall from about 88,000 in 1951 to roughly one-fourth of that number by the end of the 20th century. But in the early 21st century the number of those employed in agriculture increased to some 65,000 people, and farming was a significant contributor to Scotland's rural economy. Still, though there are thousands of crofts (subsistence farms) in the north, many of them are no longer cultivated. Crofting is a special branch of Scottish agriculture that has to be supplemented by other work, such as forestry, road work, and weaving, as well as in the tourist industry.

Most of Scotland consists of hilly or marginal land, with hill sheep farming predominating, particularly in the Southern Uplands and in the Highlands. In the southwest, dairy farming suits the wetter, milder climate and has a convenient market in the central Clydeside conurbation. The most-striking feature of livestock farming has been the rise in the number of cattle and, to a lesser extent, sheep; pig and poultry production has also expanded. However, during the 1990s, publicity surrounding an outbreak of bovine spongiform encephalopathy (commonly known as mad cow disease) adversely affected cattle farming.

Field crops are mainly found along the eastern seaboard. Barley and wheat are the main cereals; the land devoted to potatoes, though substantial, has declined. Rapeseed production has increased considerably, while oat cultivation has fallen. Oats have been replaced by barley as the main cereal for livestock feed. Malted barley is the key ingredient in Scotch whisky, a distilled liquor that is one of Scotland's best-known export products. Raspberry growing is concentrated mainly in the central eastern part of the country. Tomatoes were once grown in greenhouses in the Clyde valley, but that industry had all but vanished by the early 21st century. The output of turnips and hay for livestock feeding has fallen, replaced by an increase in grass silage.

Forestry

Forestry is a significant activity and has helped to retain population in Scotland's rural areas. Scotland is responsible for about half of the United Kingdom's total timber production and more than two-thirds of its softwood production. The forests are managed by the Forestry Commission, a public body, and by private landowners, including forestry companies. Although the Forestry Commission plants trees throughout the country, it plays a particularly important role in Highland development. The main species used are conifers, including Sitka spruce, Norway spruce, Scotch pine, European larch, and Douglas fir.

Fishing

The seafood industry has long been vital to Scotland's economy. About two-thirds of the total British fish and shellfish catch is now handled by Scottish ports. Peterhead ranks as Britain's top whitefish port, and Aberdeen and Aberdeenshire are among the United Kingdom's main centres of fish processing. Haddock, cod, herring, sole, and mackerel are the main species caught. Nephrops (langoustine) is the most important shellfish, though scallop, queen scallop, lobster, and several crab varieties are also important. Commercial salmon fishing is important on the west coast from

Argyll to the Shetland Islands, and fish farming is also important, especially of salmon and shellfish along the coast and trout in the inland lochs.

Resources and power

Mining and power generation account for less than one-tenth of Scotland's annual GDP. Until the last decade of the 20th century, Scotland's chief mineral resource was coal. The industry reached a peak annual production of 43 million tons in 1913 but subsequently declined drastically. In particular, deep mining became largely uneconomical, and Scotland's last remaining deep-pit coal mine was closed in 2002. Other minerals that have been worked intermittently include gold, silver, chromite, diatomite, and dolomite, but none has been successfully exploited. Although peat is available to a depth of 2 feet (0.6 metre) or more and is spread over some 2,650 square miles (6,880 square km), its economic value is limited. It is still burned for fuel in the Highlands, but its use has decreased because of the time and labour involved in cutting and drying it.

Britain's North Sea petroleum and natural gas resources began to be developed in the 1970s. The oil fields lie mostly in Scottish waters, but the British government holds their ownership and receives the revenue yield. Large companies have located and extracted the resource, mostly with the aid of American technology. Aberdeen is the centre of the petroleum industry, and the economy of Shetland has also benefited from discoveries in adjacent waters. In addition, natural gas from North Sea wells has replaced manufactured gas in Scotland. Tens of thousands of jobs have been created in Scotland by onshore oil- and gas-related enterprises, such as oil-platform construction and the servicing of North Sea operators. Although the newfound prosperity has been subject to the vagaries of international markets especially after fossil fuel revenues were severely reduced in the mid-

1980s the petroleum industry continues to provide, directly and indirectly, a great number of jobs in Scotland.

Water is also a valuable resource, especially for generating electricity, and several dams and power stations have been built since the mid-20th century. Coal and oil each fuel about one-fourth of Scotland's electric power stations, and nuclear generation, notably via the station at Torness, east of Edinburgh, accounts for about one-third. Almost one-fifth of Scotland's electricity is generated by renewable resources, and in the early 21st century there was an aggressive push to develop greater renewable capacity. Scotland was at the forefront of research on wave and tidal energy, and it was a global leader in the development and construction of deep-sea offshore wind farms.

Manufacturing

Manufacturing and the construction industry contribute more than one-fourth of Scotland's annual GDP. In its industrial heyday Scotland's prosperity was based on such heavy industries as coal, steel, ship construction, and engineering, but these were the industries most exposed to foreign competition and to declines in local production. The structure of Scottish industry has been gradually diversified and modernized, with a reduction in Scotland's dependence on heavy industries and replacement of them with high-technology enterprises and those making consumer goods. As with coal, the 20th-century history of steel and shipbuilding was one of reduction in the number of plants and employees.

The sale of the nationalized British Shipbuilders to the private sector accelerated the decline in the number of major shipyards in Scotland. The special facilities built to provide rigs and platforms for exploiting the North Sea oil and gas reserves have experienced fluctuating demand, and some of them have closed. Heavy industry in Scotland received a boost from the emerging wind-energy sector in the early 21st century, and the manufacture and installation of onshore and offshore turbines accounted for thousands of jobs.

Although not matching the older manufactures in terms of employment, the computer, office equipment, and electronics industries have expanded. Much of the investment in those enterprises has come from overseas, particularly from the United States. Electronics and related industries have been a major source of economic growth, employment, and export earnings. Manufacturers in the Midland Valley which has been nicknamed "Silicon Glen" because of its high-technology sector have produced many of Europe's computers and electronic machinery. Engineering industries export much of their output, and the textile industries of the Scottish Borders and the Harris tweed in the Hebrides also have a considerable, though reduced, export business.

Printing and brewing formerly were well-established industries in Edinburgh and Glasgow but are now in decline. Distilleries in the Highlands and the northeast produce the Scotch whisky for which the country is internationally famous. Whisky sales have continued to increase despite heavy taxes on home consumption. The appeal of Scotch whisky in foreign countries remains high, and whisky is one of Scotland's leading exports.

Finance

As a component of the United Kingdom, Scotland uses the British pound sterling as its official currency. Business services and banking account for a large proportion of employment in Scotland. Among the main banking and insurance jobs are legal and computer services, accountancy, and property (real estate) services. Scotland had eight joint-stock banks until the 1950s, when mergers reduced that number to three the Bank of Scotland, the Royal Bank of Scotland (RBS), and the Clydesdale Bank, each of which retains the right to issue its own notes (currency). By the 21st century RBS had become one of the world's largest financial institutions, but its ill-timed and short-lived acquisition of the Dutch bank ABN AMRO in 2007 led to the RBS's near collapse and its partial nationalization by the British government.

Financial and business services have expanded substantially since the mid-1960s, with Edinburgh becoming second in Britain only to London in this field. The banking sector also has expanded into North America and Europe. Merchant banking facilities are more widely available, and the services historically associated with Scotland, such as the management of unit and investment trusts and life funds, have expanded. About one-third of Britain's investment trusts are managed by firms in Edinburgh, Glasgow, and Dundee, which also have large investments in North America and specialized knowledge of conditions there. Unit trusts are represented in Edinburgh, where some leading British insurance companies also have their headquarters.

Services

Since the mid-1960s there has been a marked shift in employment from manufacturing to services, including tourism, with the service sector accounting for nearly four times the number of jobs as the manufacturing sector. Private services contribute about two-fifths of Scotland's GDP, whereas public services account for more than one-fifth. Retail trade is also an important job creator in Scotland.

Tourism is important in Scotland, with employment particularly strong in the hotel and catering businesses. The majority of visitors come from other parts of

Scotland or the United Kingdom, but more than two million annually come from abroad, notably the United States, Germany, France, and Ireland. Among the most popular attractions are Scotland's rural parklands, from those around Greater Glasgow and the Clyde valley to the less-accessible Highlands; the cultural institutions of Edinburgh and Glasgow; the Palace of Holyroodhouse and the country's numerous historic houses; and the Edinburgh, Stirling, Urquhart, and Blair castles. The most popular destination abroad for Scottish tourists, by far, is Spain, including the Balearic and Canary islands; additionally, many travel to other European nations and the United States.

Transportation

Public transport was formerly largely state-owned, but much of it has now been privatized. Bus services were deregulated in the 1980s, which led to greater competition, and the Scottish Transport Group, formed in 1968 to control bus and steamer services on the west coast, was dissolved in 2002. The proliferation of automobiles has made it difficult for bus companies to maintain profitable services in rural areas, where they are being either subsidized by local authorities and the government or withdrawn. Ship services from mainland ports to island towns have been curtailed and replaced by car ferries using short crossings; such ferries operate from several west coast towns to the Hebrides and other islands and from north and east coast ports to the Orkney and Shetland islands.

The Scottish road and bridge network has improved considerably, as some main routes have been upgraded to motorway standard and many single-lane roads in the Highlands have been widened. Improvements in the east and north were speeded up to cope with increased traffic generated by North Sea oil production, and bridges have been built over the Cromarty and Moray firths.

Railway services have been severely reduced since the mid-20th century, when more than 3,000 miles (4,800 km) of track were open to passenger and freight traffic. Many branchlines and stations have been closed, and the route mileage has shrunk to less than two-thirds of the former total. There has been significant electrification of Scotland's train lines, including for the suburban lines and the main line from London (Euston) to Glasgow.

Scottish ports handle many more imports than exports, as a large proportion of Britain's exports are sent abroad via English ports. Glasgow, the largest port, is under the administration of the Clyde Port Authority. The ports of Grangemouth, Dundee, and Leith, among others, are grouped under Forth Ports Limited, whereas Aberdeen is independent. Important oil ports are located in Shetland (Sullom Voe), in Orkney (Flotta), and on the east coast. Greenock and Grangemouth are equipped for container traffic, and extensive improvement schemes have been carried out at Leith and other ports. Coastal trade has dwindled because of the competition of motor transport, and inland waterways have never been a commercial success.

Air travel has increased markedly, with a substantial growth in direct services to Europe, including a large number of charter flights. Scotland has major airports at Glasgow, Edinburgh, Aberdeen, and Prestwick on the west coast, which also serves Glasgow. As Prestwick is remarkably fog-free, it is used for transatlantic flights.

Government and Society
Constitutional framework

Scotland is represented at Westminster in London by 59 members of Parliament in the House of Commons who are elected by plurality votes from single-member constituencies, and all Scottish appointive (life) peers are entitled to sit in the House of Lords. Scotland's head of government is the British prime minister, and the head of state is the British monarch. The country remains subject to the British Parliament in the areas of foreign affairs, foreign trade, defense, the national civil service, economic and monetary policy, social security, employment, energy regulation, most aspects of taxation, and some aspects of transport. The secretary of state for Scotland represents Scotland in the British government's cabinet.

Historically, the British government and its Scottish Office, headed by Scotland's secretary of state, were the sole legislative and executive authorities for Scotland. In a 1997 referendum put forward by the government of Tony Blair, nearly three-fourths of the Scottish electorate favoured the establishment of a Scottish Parliament, which formally began sitting in 1999. The Scottish Parliament, located in Edinburgh, has wide powers over such matters as health, education, housing, regional transport, the environment, and agriculture. It also has the power to increase or decrease the British income tax rate by 3 percent within Scotland. The leading parliamentary party or coalition appoints the Scottish Executive, the administrative arm of the government, which is headed by a first minister.

Local government

Local authorities in Scotland are administrative bodies that must act within the framework of laws passed by the European, United Kingdom, and Scottish parliaments. They are responsible for a range of community services, including environmental matters, urban planning, education, roadways and traffic, firefighting, sanitation, housing, parks and recreation, and elections.

Scotland is divided into 32 council areas, each administered by a local council. The council areas vary considerably in both geographic extent and population. Highland is the largest council area, encompassing 10,091 square miles (26,136 square km), and, at 25 square miles (65 square km), Dundee is the smallest. With a population of roughly 600,000 people, Glasgow is the most populous council area, whereas the least populous is the Orkney Islands, which has about 20,000 residents.

Within the local council areas are hundreds of communities, including towns, villages, and city neighbourhoods. Communities may elect community councils to serve on a voluntary basis and perform a mainly consultative role. Their concerns include environmental and planning matters affecting their communities.

Justice

Scotland has a distinct legal and judicial system that is based on Roman law. The country is divided into six sheriffdoms (Glasgow; Grampian Highland and Islands; Lothian and Borders; North Strathclyde; South Strathclyde, Dumfries, and Galloway; and Tayside, Central, and Fife), each with a sheriff principal (chief judge) and a varying number of sheriffs. There are 49 sheriff courts divided among the sheriffdoms. The most serious offenses triable by jury are reserved for the High Court of Justiciary, the supreme court for criminal cases. The judges are the same as those of the Court of Session, the supreme court for civil cases. An appeal may be directed to the Supreme Court of the United Kingdom from the Court of Session but not from the High Court of Justiciary. The Court of Session, consisting of the lord president, the lord justice clerk, and 22 other judges, sits in Edinburgh and is divided into an Outer House, which hears cases at first instance, and an Inner House, which hears appeals from the Outer House and from lower courts. The Inner House has two divisions, each with six judges. The sheriff courts have a wide jurisdiction in civil cases, but certain actions, such as challenging governmental decisions, are reserved for the Court of Session. They also deal with most criminal offenses, with serious cases tried by jury. The decision whether to prosecute is made by the lord advocate in the High Court and by procurators fiscal in the sheriff courts. District courts, presided over by lay judges, deal with minor criminal offenses. There is also a system for hearing cases involving children.

The lord advocate and the solicitor general for Scotland are the Scottish Executive's law officers, charged with representing the Scottish government in court cases. The lord advocate also serves as Scotland's public prosecutor. Both are appointed by the British monarch on the recommendation of the first minister and with the approval of the Scottish Parliament. The advocate general for Scotland, who is the law officer of the United Kingdom responsible for Scottish matters, acts as an adviser to the British government and to the Scottish lord advocate and solicitor general.

Political process

All citizens at least 18 years of age are eligible to vote. Voters in Scotland elect representatives to local councils, the Scottish Parliament, the British House of Commons, and the European Parliament. Terms of office vary for elected officials. Local councillors serve three-year terms, and members of the House of Commons and European Parliament serve five-year terms. Historically, members of the Scottish Parliament have served four-year terms, but that term was extended to five years in 2016 so that the Scottish parliamentary election originally scheduled for May 2020 would not conflict with the similarly scheduled election for the House of Commons. (Whether the term would continue to be five years after the 2021 election for the Scottish Parliament remained to be determined.) Although local, Scottish, and European elections take place at regular intervals, elections to the House of Commons occur at least once every five years, with the date set by the British government. Non-British European Union citizens are eligible to participate in local and European Parliament elections.

There are 129 members of the Scottish Parliament; 73 are chosen from single-member constituencies and 56 by proportional representation from regional party lists. Coalition governments between the Scottish Labour Party and the Scottish Liberal Democrats were necessary in the initial sittings of the Parliament, as no single party was able to win a majority in the Scottish Parliament. In 2007, however, the Scottish National Party (SNP) formed a minority administration.

Until the middle of the 20th century, Scottish voters split their loyalties about evenly between the Conservative (traditionally known in Scotland as the Scottish Conservative and Unionist Party) and Labour parties, but thereafter into the early 21st century the Labour Party dominated Scottish politics. Indeed, at the 1997 national election the Conservative Party returned no members to the House of Commons. From Keir Hardie, who cofounded the Independent Labour Party in the 1890s, to Ramsay MacDonald, Labour's first prime minister, in the 1920s, to Prime Minister Tony Blair and his successor, Gordon Brown, in the 1990s and early 21st century, many of the most influential Labour Party politicians have either been Scottish-born or resided in Scotland. The Liberal Democrats have maintained fairly strong support in the Celtic fringes of Scotland, and the SNP, which advocates Scotland's independence from the United Kingdom, has captured a significant share of support since the 1970s. In the 2007 elections the SNP narrowly won the most seats in the Scottish Parliament, but it secured a clear majority in 2011 as Labour continued to rebuild and support for the Liberal Democrats virtually collapsed.

Security

Military planning in Scotland is the responsibility of the British government. Scotland is the site of a number of key military installations, including several belonging to the North Atlantic Treaty Organization (NATO). The Royal Navy has a base at Rosyth on the Firth of Forth, and the Royal Air Force has stations at Lossiemouth and Leuchars. Scottish infantry regiments are still distinguished by their tartans: kilts for the Highland regiments and trousers for those of the Lowlands. The oldest infantry regiment in the British army is the Royal Scots.

The Scottish Parliament and the Scottish Executive have a general responsibility for law and order. In 2013 Scotland's eight local police forces were merged into a single national force. As in England and Wales, the police do not normally carry firearms, although special units carry guns when dealing with armed or particularly dangerous criminals.

Health and welfare

Health care in Scotland is provided mostly free of charge through the National Health Service. The

Scottish Parliament is responsible for health, welfare services, and housing. Scotland's 14 health boards are accountable to the Scottish Executive through the minister for health. The country has some of the highest incidences in Europe of heart disease and lung cancer, which are among the leading causes of death in Scotland, along with other types of cancer and diseases of the respiratory, circulatory, and digestive systems.

Housing

Home ownership in Scotland generally has lagged behind that of the rest of the United Kingdom. Because of policies implemented by the government of Margaret Thatcher in the 1980s that encouraged home ownership, owner-occupied units increased from barely two-fifths of total housing in the mid-1980s to two-thirds in the early 21st century. Local housing authorities provide about one-fifth of the housing units in Scotland. The housing stock in Scotland varies considerably in size and type. In the latter part of the 20th century, several government-subsidized housing complexes were built on the outskirts of urban areas; however, many of those properties have since become owner-occupied or have been taken over by housing trusts.

Education

Scotland's education system is rooted in tradition. Schools run by the church existed in the Middle Ages, and by the end of the 15th century Scotland already had three universities. Towns were involved in founding schools by the 16th century, and during the 17th century the old Scottish Parliament passed several acts encouraging the establishment of schools. Scotland retained its separate education system following the Act of Union in 1707, and it developed considerably over the next 200 years. In the early 20th century Scotland introduced a single external examination system, founded new secondary schools, and replaced school boards with local education authorities. The state also took over responsibility for Roman Catholic primary and secondary schools; however, the Roman Catholic Church has continued to influence staffing, religious education, and the general ethos of the schools.

The educational system in Scotland was markedly reformed in the 1960s, notably by switching from selective to comprehensive secondary schools. The vocational education system also rapidly expanded during this period, and the number of universities increased from four to eight (St. Andrews, Glasgow, Aberdeen, Edinburgh, Strathclyde, Heriot-Watt, Dundee, and Stirling). New standards were enacted in the 1970s and '80s in an effort to promote further reform and to give parents a greater say in the education of their children. The number of universities increased again in the 1990s as some existing institutions were accorded university status.

Early education is optional and is provided in nursery schools, day nurseries, and play groups, as well as through private child care and other arrangements. The government has a policy of guaranteeing a nursery place to every child age four or five, partially as a means of helping mothers who wish to return to paid employment. School education is compulsory and is provided free for all children between the ages of 5 and 16. Parents have the right to send their children to the school of their choice, although there are some restrictions on this right. Parents can also choose to send their children to private, fee-paying schools.

Unlike in England, there is no national curriculum, but the "Curriculum for Excellence" practices were introduced in the 21st century to provide a framework for such matters. Students transfer from primary to secondary school at about the age of 12, and nearly three-fourths continue their studies beyond the school-leaving age of 16. Postsecondary education is available in further-education colleges or higher-education institutions. Further-education colleges provide vocational education and training and also offer a range of higher-education courses.

Education from preschool to higher education is one of the responsibilities of the Scottish Parliament. Policies are administered through the Education and Lifelong Learning Department. Many aspects of educational administration are devolved to education authorities and to schools themselves, and further- and higher-education institutions are responsible for much of their own administration. The Scottish Further and Higher Education Funding Council (formed in 2005 from the amalgamation of the Scottish Higher Education Funding Council and the Scottish Further Education

Funding Council) plays a key role in allocating funds to institutions in these sectors.

Local authorities are responsible for providing schooling, special educational needs, and the (legally guaranteed) provision of Gaelic teaching in Gaelic-speaking areas. They are also responsible for creating plans that set out a framework for the development of community education in their areas. School boards also play a role in the provision of public education and allow for the election of parents and for their input in the running of their children's school. Both the Roman Catholic Church and the Church of Scotland have the right of representation on local-authority education committees.

Private education is provided outside the state system, and independent or "public" schools, as they are known vary considerably in size. Some public schools focus on primary- or secondary-age pupils, while others offer a complete education from preschool to age 18. The highest concentration of public schools is found in Edinburgh.

Cultural and Tradition

Scotland's culture and customs remain remarkably vigorous and distinctive despite the country's union with the United Kingdom since the early 18th century and the threat of dominance by its more powerful partner to the south. Its strength springs in part from the diverse strands that make up its background, including European mainstream cultures. It has also been enriched by contacts with Europe, owing to the mobility of the Scottish people since the Middle Ages and the hospitality of Scotland's universities to foreign students and faculty.

What is it that makes the Scots Scottish? And if you think of Scotland or its inhabitants what is the first thing that springs to mind? The history and the clans perhaps? The beautiful landscape? The castles? The bagpipes? The Highland Games? Or is it whisky? Fact is that you are likely to find some unique features in Scotland and its people that you won't find easily, and originally, anywhere else in the world. For most outsiders Scotland is about clans, battles, kilts, tartan etc. It must be said though that this image is up to a certain point valid for the Highland-Gaelic area but doesn't include the lowlands of Scotland although most people, and specially the tourist agents, want us to belief that. But let's start with the typical images some of us have and deal with the other things that make the Scots Scottish later.

Highland/Gaelic Culture

Many years ago the ruggedness of the land led to the separation of the Highlanders into small groups called clans. Each clan was ruled by a chief, and the members of a clan claimed descent from a common ancestor. The traditional garment of the Highland clansmen is the kilt (belted plaid), which is suitable for climbing the rough hills. Each clan had its own colourful pattern for weaving cloth and these patterns are called a tartan. Nowadays the kilt is no longer a historic dress but a national costume, proudly worn for special occasions such as weddings etc. I have heard that there are currently over 4,500 different tartans and you can even have your own tartan if you like. Visit one of the many Woollen Mills you'll find all over Scotland for some tartan related products. The most renowned one is probably the Edinburgh Woollen Mill at the beginning of the Royal Mile.

The clans aren't something from the past, they are still here today. Currently there are more than 500 active clans registered all over the world and they all play an important role in maintaining and celebrating the Scottish traditions. There are annually more than 100 gatherings of the clans, which draw many visitors to the Highlands.

Highland Games

Despite their name, Highland Games are held all over Scotland, From Spring To late Autumn: they vary in size and differ in the range of events they offer, and although the most famous are at Oban, Cowal and especially Braemar, often the smaller ones are more fun.

The Highland Games probably originated in the fourteenth century as a means of recruiting the best fighting men for the clan chiefs, and were popularised by Queen Victoria to encourage the traditional dress, music, games and dance of the highlands, various royals still attend the games at Braemar.

The most distinctive events are know as the heavies tossing the caber, putting the stone, and tossing the weight over the bar, all of which require prodigious strength and skill. Tossing the caber is the most spectacular and the most well known event in the highland games, when the athlete must run carrying an entire tree trunk and attempt to heave is end over end in a perfect, elegant throw.

Just as important as the sporting events are the piping competitions for individuals and bands and dancing competitions where you will see young children tripping the quick, intricate steps of such traditional dances as the Highland fling.

When on holiday in Scotland the Highland games should not be missed and will give you a great insight of Scottish traditions, and leave you with many memories of a great day.

Highland Dress

At formal occasions the Scots proudly wear their Highland Dress which consists of a kilt and other pieces of clothing depending on the occasion. The Scottish kilt is usually worn with kilt hose (woollen socks), turned down at the knee, often with garter flashes, and a sporran (a type of pouch), which hangs around the waist from a chain or leather strap. This may be plain or embossed leather, or decorated with sealskin, fur, or polished metal plating. Other accessories which are often used are a belt with embossed buckle, Argyll jacket, a kilt pin and a black knife worn in the top of the right hose.

Bagpipes

Scotland is often associated with bagpipes but the interesting fact is that bagpipes aren't originally from Scotland. Bagpipes originate from southern Europe and appear in Scotland around 1400 AD. The Scottish

Bagpipe, or Great Highland Bagpipe, became established in the British military and achieved the widespread prominence it enjoys today, whereas other bagpipe traditions throughout Europe, ranging from Spain to Russia, almost universally went into decline by the late 19th and early 20th centuries. Though widely famous for its role in military and civilian pipe bands, the Great Highland Bagpipe is also used for a solo virtuosic style called pibroch. If you're interested you can visit the annual Glasgow International Piping Festival which is held in August.

Now that I have written about the image most tourists have of Scotland it's time to realise that Scots are also just people like you and me and are not running around over the hills in kilts all day. They are a usually very friendly bunch and are fortunate to live in a beautiful country of which they are very proud of, and for a good reason I might add. The rich history, the unpredictable climate and the dramatic landscape plays an important part in daily life, specially if you consider that many Scots earn their living in the tourism industry.

Food and Drink

Haggis is Scotland's national dish, although a good curry comes in second and for some even in the first place. Haggis is a dish containing sheep's 'pluck' (heart, liver and lungs), minced with onion, oatmeal, suet, spices, and salt, mixed with stock, and traditionally simmered in the animal's stomach for approximately three hours. If it's prepared properly it's a real treat! Haggis is traditionally served with the Burns supper at January 25th or thereabouts, when Scotland's national poet, Robert Burns, is commemorated. He wrote the poem Address to a Haggis, which starts "Fair fa' your honest, sonsie face, Great chieftain o' the puddin-race!" and is usually proceeded by a piper.

Apart from the Haggis, Scotland has many other delicious dishes on offer and one of the most bizarre things you can buy in some Scottish fish and chip shops are, besides fish and chips of course, deep fried mars bars. Whether this is a treat or not I'm not sure, fact is that they are not good for your health but seem to taste surprisingly well! If you want to try something different go for an Arbroath Smokie, a specially smoked type of Haddock and the name is protected by EU regulations. Arbroath Smokies originate in Auchmithie, a small fishing village a few miles north of Arbroath, on the Scottish east coast. If you think whisky is the only national drink you're wrong. There is also Irn-Bru, a carbonated fruit flavoured soft drink, which also carries the title of Scottish National Drink, or perhaps better the "other" national drink. Another typical Scottish thing is Shortbread, a buttery biscuit, available almost anywhere and specially in the tourist shops! Read more in our Scottish Food Guide.

Ceilidh

If you are staying in Scotland you are likely to hear about a ceilidh, specially if you stay in the more traditional Highland hotels or smaller villages. A ceilidh is a traditional Gaelic social gathering, usually held in village halls and hotels, and involves playing folk music and dancing and this is very much the case today. In the old days it was literary entertainment where stories and tales were rehearsed and recited, and songs were sung. A ceilidh can be good fun and entertaining and you can also work on your traditional Scottish dances which come in many forms and paces to suite both the young and the old. Attending one is a must when you are holidaying in Scotland.

Religion

After you've spent the Friday or Saturday evening partying at a ceilidh or visited one of the many pleasant pubs and bars you are likely to find out on

Sunday that religion plays an important part in Scotland. The Scottish Presbyterians is the official, as well as the largest, church in the country. The Church of Scotland, as it is called, claims the adherence of nearly half the population. Roman Catholics, particularly strong in the western Highlands, make up the second-largest group of worshippers. After the church visit on Sunday morning you'll find out something that isn't at all common in other European countries, the Sunday Paper. Don't be surprised when visiting a local shop in the Highlands that around two o'clock it suddenly becomes very crowded. The reason for that is the arrival of the Sunday Paper, bought by many and often accompanied with a (wee) bottle of the national drink! While most of the readers go back home, others regard this as an opportunity to visit the local pub and meet their friends.

Sports and recreation

For many (overseas) tourists Scotland is renowned for being the "Home of Golf" and many visitors are very keen to play the famous links at St. Andrews in Fife. For the Scots themselves soccer is the national passion and beating England the most important goal, and this is not only in soccer... Also famous in soccer is "The Old Firm", a common collective name for Celtic and Rangers, both football clubs from Glasgow. Whereas Celtic's fans are mostly catholic, the Rangers fans are mostly protestant. The competition between the two clubs is fierce and often leads to violence between rivalling supporters, not only on match day. Both teams usually meet four times a year in the Scottish Premier League. Other popular sports include hill-walking, rugby, shinty, lawn-bowling, fishing, darts and curling. The island of Ailsa Craig, off the Ayrshire coast, provides the special granite for most of the curling stones.

It's hard to write everything down that's related to Scottish Culture, otherwise it would become an endless page. You will find that much of the Scottish culture and traditions are saved in the many festivals that are held annually, all over the country and all year round and perhaps especially during Hogmanay. The best thing to do is go out there, spend some time in one place, visit the pubs and ceilidhs, experience some of the festivals and other events and try to get to know the locals a bit better. That's how you discover for yourself what the Scots and their culture are all about and you will be pleasantly surprised.

Sports are an important part of life in Scotland. Association football (soccer) has a wide following and is dominated by the Rangers and Celtic clubs of Glasgow. Rugby football is played especially by private schools and by their former pupils, but in the towns of the Scottish Borders it draws players and spectators from a wider social range. Although Scottish athletes compete as members of the United Kingdom's Olympic team, the country fields national teams for other sports (e.g., football and rugby). Shinty, a hockeylike game, is popular in the Highlands. Curling is another traditional sport, although temperatures are seldom low enough for it to be other than an indoor activity played on man-made ice. Golf, long associated with Scotland though its origins lie elsewhere, is accessible to most Scots through widespread public and private facilities, and the country hosts one of professional golf's most prestigious tournaments, the annual Open Championship (also known outside of Great Britain as the British Open).

The Old Course of the Royal and Ancient Golf Club of St. Andrews in Fife is the most famous of many excellent seaside courses. Scotland's landscape is ideally suited to those pursuing hill walking, rock climbing, sailing, and canoeing. Skiing facilities have been developed in the Cairngorms and other areas.

Hunting and shooting are traditionally sports of the wealthy, but fishing is popular among all classes, and the country boasts some of the finest salmon fishing in the world. (For further discussion, see United Kingdom: Cultural life.)

Daily life and social customs

Although bagpipes have ancient origins elsewhere and are found throughout the world, they are one of the most recognized symbols of Scottish culture. By the 16th century, various clans had established hereditary pipers, and later the instrument was used in wartime to inflame the passions of soldiers in battle. The form of the kilt, Scotland's national costume, has evolved since the emigration of Scots from Ireland. The modern kilt, with its tartan pattern, became common in the 18th century and served an important role in the formation of a Scottish national identity. Knits from

Fair Isle, with their distinctive designs woven from the fine wool of Shetland sheep, are also world famous.

One traditional local custom is the ceilidh (visit), a social occasion that includes music and storytelling. Once common throughout the country, the ceilidh is now a largely rural institution. Sports such as tossing the caber (a heavy pole) and the hammer throw are integral to the Highland games, a spectacle that originated in the 19th century; the games are accompanied by pipe bands and (usually solo) performances by Highland dancers. Other traditions include Burns suppers (honouring poet Robert Burns), which often feature haggis (a delicacy traditionally consisting of offal and suet boiled with oatmeal in a sheep's stomach) and cock-a-leekie (chicken stewed with leeks).

Many Scots consider these games and traditions to be a self-conscious display of legendary characteristics that have little to do with ordinary Scottish life a show put on, like national costumes, to gratify the expectations of tourists and encouraged by the royal family's annual appearance at the Braemar Gathering near Balmoral Castle. Scottish country dancing, however, is a pastime whose popularity has spread far beyond Scotland.

Food and drink have played a central role in Scotland's heritage. In addition to haggis, Scotland is known for its Angus beef, porridge, stovies (a potato-rich stew), shortbreads, scones, cheese (Bishop, Kennedy, Caboc, Lanark Blue), toffee, and game dishes (e.g., salmon, venison, and grouse). The term whisky is derived from the Gaelic uisge-beatha, meaning "water of life." Historical references to whisky date from the late 15th century, though its popularity in the country probably goes back even farther. Indeed, throughout Scotland private distilleries proliferated in the 17th century, which led the Scottish Parliament to impose a tax on whisky production in 1644. Today whisky is among the country's leading exports.

The arts

As well as being a country steeped in history and heritage, Scotland also has a vibrant arts, culture and entertainment scene. From world-famous actors and musicians to world-class artists and writers, Scotland is a small nation brimming with talent. Our long and exciting history also means we offer some of the world's best museums and galleries, with many of them free to enter.

Music is ingrained within the history of Scotland. Some of the world's most popular modern music groups and artists hail from Scotland, including Belle & Sebastian, Snow Patrol and Susan Boyle. What's more, our three internationally-renowned classical orchestras mean there's no shortage of classical talent here either.

Scotland's rich heritage in music and performance makes it the perfect place to enjoy theatre, dance and opera. A number of festivals every year, including the world-famous Festival Fringe and International Festivals, take place in Edinburgh during the summer, showcasing both established and emerging talents from across the globe.

Scotland is also a major player in the film industry. We might not have much in common with Hollywood, but perhaps that's why our rolling hills and serene landscapes have proved so popular with film crews over the past decade. The booming Scottish film industry has attracted such stars as Brad Pitt, Scarlett Johansson and Daniel Craig to our shores.

We're not short on stars in the world of fashion and design, either. World famous fashion designers, including Jonathan Saunders, Graeme Black, and Holly Fulton, to name just a few, are the finest of Scotland's crop. On top of this, our internationally-renowned architects, such as Charles Rennie Mackintosh and William Henry Playfair, have played a large part in making Scottish cities as beautiful as they are today.

Scottish writers have the choice of three languages English, Scots, and Gaelic. An early Scottish poet of the 16th century, Sir Robert Ayton, wrote in standard English; one of his poems is thought to have inspired Robert Burns's version of "Auld Lang Syne." Burns is perhaps the foremost literary figure in Scottish history. A poet whose songs were written in the Scottish dialect of English, Burns aroused great passion among his audience and gained a legion of dedicated followers.

Hugh MacDiarmid, a nationalist and Marxist, gained an international reputation for his Scots poetry in the first half of the 20th century, and others, such as Robert Garioch and Edwin Muir, followed his lead. Gaelic poets such as Sorley Maclean and Derick Thompson are highly esteemed, as is Iain Crichton Smith, who is also known for his novels in English. Other contemporary novelists, many of whom earned an international following, include Muriel Spark, Alasdair Gray, Ian Rankin, Kate Atkinson, and James Kelman. Alexander McCall Smith, who moved to Edinburgh, was made famous by his detective stories set in Botswana. Similarly, the Harry Potter books were written in Edinburgh by English novelist J.K. Rowling.

Painting and sculpture flourish and are displayed in numerous galleries and official exhibitions. In the late 20th century there was a popular revival of 19th-century designer and architect Charles Rennie Mackintosh.

Scots have also made their mark in motion pictures. Sean Connery, perhaps best known for his portrayal of James Bond, was Scotland's most-recognizable film star of the second half of the 20th century. Actors Ewan

McGregor and Gerard Butler became familiar screen presences in the early 21st century. Glaswegian stand-up comedian and actor Billy Connolly was a major force in British entertainment since the 1970s.

Director Bill Forsyth first gained international acclaim in the 1980s, and his 1983 film Local Hero prompted a wave of tourism to the western islands. Scottish filmmaking also enjoyed a renaissance after the success of Braveheart (1995), an American production that chronicles Scottish battles with the English in the 13th century and that helped rekindle nationalist aspirations. Other films, such as Trainspotting (1996), Orphans (1997), Young Adam (2003), and Red Road (2006), enjoyed wide success, and Scottish films now figure in many international festivals.

Scotland has a wealth of surviving traditional music, ranging from the work songs of the Hebrides to the ballads of the northeast. There has also been renewed interest in such traditional instruments as the bagpipe, fiddle, and clarsach (the small Celtic harp). Performers such as the Battlefield Band, Tannahill Weavers, and Dougie MacLean have brought Scottish folk music to international audiences. Scotland has also had a long presence in popular music, with artists such as Lonnie Donegan, a pioneer of prerock skiffle music, singer-songwriter Donovan, the Incredible String Band, and the Eurythmics. Whereas many Scots had to leave the country to find success, vibrant local scenes in Glasgow and Edinburgh in the 1980s gave rise to such popular groups as Simple Minds and the Jesus and Mary Chain and later to Teenage Fanclub, Travis, Belle and Sebastian, and Snow Patrol.

Support for the Arts. The Scottish Arts Council is advised by specialist committees about funding for theaters, art galleries, musical and literary organizations, art centers, and major festivals. Almost half the budget goes to support the four national companies: Scottish Opera, Scottish Ballet, Royal National Orchestra, and Scottish Chamber Orchestra. Local authorities and economic development agencies have become major contributors. In the popular arts, self-financing and ticket charges are important.

Literature. Passion for the spoken word has arisen from linguistic diversity and the tradition of public oration and dispute on scriptural subjects. The ability to tell a good story or joke is prized. There are rich poetry and prose traditions in Gaelic, Scots, and Scots-inflected English. Gaelic literature derives from bardic verses celebrating heroes and political leaders. The development of Gaelic communities in the major cities, particularly Glasgow, around 1870–1914 stimulated new linguistic and literary awareness.

Scottish literature oscillates between romantic flourishes and mordant commentary, often suggesting a preoccupation with dialectical tensions: reason-passion, reality fantasy, natural-supernatural, solemnity-satire. There was a notable revival after the World War I, spearheaded by the poet Hugh MacDiarmid. Many twentieth century prose writers wrote about Scottish locales and themes. Recent works such as Alasdair Gray's *Lanark* and Irvine Welsh's *Trainspotting* combine gritty reality and wild imagination with Scots language and caustic visions of a deindustrializing world.

Graphic Arts. Scottish painting has struggled to establish a distinctive identity. Scottishness has been a question of subject matter more than style. Since 1900, French impressionism and post-1960s conceptual approaches have been influential. The absence of a major Scottish-based art market has tended to keep the fine arts semiprofessional.

Stylized animals and objects in bas relief on Pictish symbol stones mixed with the curvilinear designs of

Celtic Christianity in the first millennium C.E. French and Flemish influences appear in medieval church sculpture. In the nineteenth century, neoclassical styles dominated. Only with the rise of modernism has the long connection between architecture and ornamental sculpture been broken, allowing freer, more experimental modes to develop.

At a more popular and functional level, jewelry and textiles sustain artistic traditions that often allude to Pictish and Celtic design themes. Major art colleges provide support, particularly in the area of textiles.

Performance Arts. The national ballet, opera, and orchestras and the Edinburgh festival ensure that a high art tradition is maintained. Traditional music and dance have had a revival, sustained by dedicated groups and associations, major nationwide competitive events, and a tradition of informal music-making in pubs, along with the new popularity of the Ceilidh, a public event of traditional set dances to fiddle tunes. There is an active folk scene, and a strong popular music scene. Since the 1970s there has been a flourishing of new theaters and companies performing new works in Scots and translations of plays into that language.

The State of the Physical and Social Sciences

Scotland was in the forefront of the development of the physical and social sciences, including groundbreaking work in the eighteenth century in mathematics by Colin MacLaurin, geology by James Hutton, and in chemistry by Joseph Black, sociological data gathering in the Statistical Account (1790s), and the moral philosophy and political economy of David Hume, Adam Smith, John Millar, and Adam Ferguson.

During the heyday of industrialization, Scotland became preeminent in the field of engineering, and the social sciences were eclipsed by the physical sciences, exemplified by the physicists Lord Kelvin (William Thomson) and James Clark Maxwell. The sciences atrophied during the post-World War I industrial decline. Since the 1960s, there has been a push to strengthen the role of physical sciences in higher education. Technology transfer between industry and university has been a core goal, supported by the establishment of university-associated research institutes. Offshore engineering, aquaculture, veterinary medicine, and computers are key research areas along with medicine. Scotland has been a leader in cloning research, and the school of linguistics at Edinburgh has stimulated work on the interface of speech and computers.

Whereas corporate funding has provided major support for the physical sciences, the social sciences have had to compete for funds from the Economic and Social Research Council and smaller sources. Political change has stimulated revivals in history and legal studies and reestablished Scotland as a topic for political and sociological study.

Cultural institutions

All of the arts receive support from Creative Scotland (formed when the Scottish Arts Council joined Scottish Screen in 2010). All aspects of traditional culture are researched, archived, and taught in the Department of Celtic and Scottish Studies of the University of Edinburgh.

Edinburgh and Glasgow are the cultural capitals of Scotland. Among the cultural institutions achieving high international standing are the Royal Scottish National Orchestra, the Scottish Opera, and the Scottish Ballet, all based in Glasgow. Other major institutions in Glasgow include the Kelvingrove Art Gallery and Museum, the Burrell Collection, and the Riverside Museum, The National Museums of Scotland include the National Museum and the War Museum in

Edinburgh, the Museum of Rural Life near Glasgow, the Museum of Flight near Haddington, and the Museum of Costume at Shambellie House near Dumfries. Edinburgh is also the headquarters of the National Library of Scotland, which receives copies of all books published in the United Kingdom and Ireland, and the National Galleries of Scotland, comprising several museums, including the National Gallery of Scotland (with works by Allan Ramsay, Sir Henry Raeburn, and other Scottish painters), the Scottish National Portrait Gallery, and the Scottish National Gallery of Modern Art. Founded in 1947, the annual Edinburgh International Festival, with its Fringe (entertainment on the periphery of the festival), has become one of the world's largest cultural events.

Media and publishing

Edinburgh was once one of the centres of the United Kingdom's publishing industry. However, in the early and mid-20th century, Scottish publishing declined drastically, especially in the years after World War II, with many publishers moving to London. Only in the 1970s did Scotland's publishing industry begin to revitalize somewhat. Some newspapers are printed in Scotland, but others, which include aspects of Scottish news and sports, are delivered from south of the border.

The Daily Record and The Scottish Sun have the largest circulation in Scotland. The Herald (Glasgow) and The Scotsman (Edinburgh) continue to serve the west and east coasts, respectively, and their Sunday equivalents, the Sunday Herald and Scotland on Sunday, are competitors. Other parts of Scotland are served by local papers such as the Dundee Courier and The Press and Journal. Scottish Field and Scots Magazine are two well-established monthly publications covering traditional, leisure, and historical interests.

The British Broadcasting Corporation (BBC) produces Scottish news and other programming for radio and television, including some broadcasts in Gaelic. Radio Scotland has largely locally produced programs. There are three independent television companies, including Scottish Television (STV), and several independent radio stations. Somewhat controversially, the Westminster Parliament has retained legislative powers over broadcasting.

History

Ancient times

Evidence of human settlement in the area later known as Scotland dates from the 3rd millennium bc. The earliest people, Mesolithic (Middle Stone Age) hunters and fishermen who probably reached Scotland via an ancient land bridge from the Continent, were to be found on the west coast, near Oban, and as far south as Kirkcudbright, where their settlements are marked by large deposits of discarded mollusk shells. Remains suggest that settlers at the Forth estuary, in the area of modern Stirling, obtained meat from stranded whales.

By early in the 2nd millennium bc, Neolithic (New Stone Age) farmers had begun cultivating cereals and keeping cattle and sheep. They made settlements on the west coast and as far north as Shetland. Many built collective chamber tombs, such as the Maeshowe barrow in Orkney, which is the finest example in Britain. A settlement of such people at Skara Brae in Orkney consists of a cluster of seven self-contained huts connected by covered galleries or alleys. The "Beaker folk," so called from the shape of their drinking vessels, migrated to eastern Scotland from northern Europe, probably beginning about 1800 bc. They buried their dead in individual graves and were pioneers in bronze working. The most impressive monuments of Bronze Age Scotland are the stone circles, presumably for religious ceremonies, such as those at Callanish in Lewis and Brodgar in Orkney, the latter being more than 300 feet (90 metres) in diameter.

From about 700 bc onward there was a distinct final period in Scottish prehistory. This period is the subject of current archaeological controversy, with somewhat less stress than in the past being placed on the importance of the introduction of iron fabrication or on the impact of large new groups of iron-using settlers. One key occurrence in the middle of the 1st millennium was the change from a relatively warm and dry climate to one that was cooler and wetter.

In terms of technology, this period was marked by the appearance of hill forts, defensive structures having stone ramparts with an internal frame of timber; a good example is at Abernethy near the Tay. Some of these forts have been dated to the 7th and 6th centuries bc, which might suggest that they were adopted by already established tribes rather than introduced by incomers. Massive decorated bronze armlets with Celtic ornamentation, found in northeastern Scotland and dated to the period ad 50–

150, suggest that chieftains from outside may have gone to these tribes at this period, displaced from farther south first by fresh settlers from the Continent and later by the Romans in ad 43.

From 100 bc the "brochs" appeared in the extreme north of Scotland and the northern isles. These were high, round towers, which at Mousa in Shetland stand almost 50 feet (15 metres) in height. The broch dwellers may have carried on intermittent warfare with the fort builders of farther south. On the other hand, the two types of structures may not represent two wholly distinct cultures, and the two peoples may have together constituted the ancestors of the people later known as the Picts.

The houses of these people were circular, sometimes standing alone and sometimes in groups of 15 or more, as at Hayhope Knowe in the Cheviot Hills on the border between modern Scotland and England. Some single steadings, set in bogs or on lakesides, are called crannogs. Grain growing was probably of minor importance in the economy; the people were pastoralists and food gatherers. They were ruled by a warrior aristocracy whose bronze and iron parade equipment has, in a few instances, survived.

Roman penetration

Gnaeus Julius Agricola, the Roman governor of Britain from ad 77 to 84, was the first Roman general to operate extensively in Scotland. He defeated the native population at Mons Graupius, possibly in Banffshire, probably in ad 84. In the following year he was recalled, and his policy of containing the hostile tribes within the Highland zone, which he had marked by building a legionary fortress at Inchtuthil in Strathmore, was not continued. His tactics were logical if Scotland was to be subdued but probably required the commitment of more troops than the overall strategy of the Roman Empire could afford. The only other period in which a forward policy was attempted was between about 144 and about 190, when a turf wall, the Antonine Wall (named for the emperor Antoninus Pius), was manned between the Forth and the Clyde.

The still-impressive stone structure known as Hadrian's Wall had been built between the Tyne and Solway Firth between 122 and 128, and it was to be the permanent northern frontier of Roman Britain. After a northern uprising, the emperor Severus supervised the restoring of the Hadrianic line from 209 to 211, and thereafter southeastern Scotland seems to have enjoyed almost a century of peace. In the 4th century there were successive raids from north of the wall and periodic withdrawals of Roman troops to continental Europe. Despite increasing use of native buffer states in front of the wall, the Romans found their frontier indefensible by the end of the 4th century.

At Housesteads, at about the midpoint of Hadrian's Wall, archaeologists have uncovered a market where northern natives exchanged cattle and hides for Roman products; in this way some Roman wares, and possibly more general cultural influences, found their way north, but the scale of this commerce was probably small. Roman civilization, typified by the towns and villas, or country houses, of southern Britain, was unknown in Scotland, which as a whole was never dominated by the Romans or even strongly influenced by them.

From about ad 400 there was a long period for which written evidence is scanty. Four peoples the Picts, the Scots, the Britons, and the Angles were eventually to merge and thus form the kingdom of Scots.

The Picts occupied Scotland north of the Forth. Their identity has been much debated, but they possessed a distinctive culture, seen particularly in their carved symbol stones. Their original language, presumably non-Indo-European, has disappeared; some Picts probably spoke a Brythonic Celtic language. Pictish unity may have been impaired by their apparent tradition of matrilineal succession to the throne.

The Scots, from Dalriada in northern Ireland, colonized the Argyll area, probably in the late 5th century. Their continuing connection with Ireland was a source of strength to them, and Scottish and Irish Gaelic (Goidelic Celtic languages) did not become distinct from each other until the late Middle Ages. Scottish Dalriada soon extended its cultural as well as its military sway east and south, though one of its greatest kings, Aidan, was defeated by the Angles in 603 at Degsastan near the later Scottish border.

The Britons, speaking a Brythonic Celtic language, colonized Scotland from farther south, probably from the 1st century bc onward. They lost control of southeastern Scotland to the Angles in the early 7th century ad. The British heroic poem Gododdin describes a stage in this process. The British kingdom of Strathclyde in southwestern Scotland remained, with its capital at Dumbarton.

The Angles were Teutonic-speaking invaders from across the North Sea. Settling from the 5th century, they had by the early 7th century created the kingdom of Northumbria, stretching from the Humber to the Forth. A decisive check to their northward advance was administered in 685 by the Picts at the Battle of Nechtansmere in Angus.

Christianity

Christianity was introduced to Scotland in late Roman times, and traditions of the evangelizing of St. Ninian in the southwest have survived. He is a shadowy figure, however, and it is doubtful that his work extended very far north.

Firmly established throughout Scotland by the Celtic clergy, Christianity came with the Scots settlers from Ireland and possibly gave them a decisive cultural advantage in the early unification of kingdoms. The Celtic church lacked a territorial organization of parishes and dioceses and a division between secular and regular clergy; its communities of missionary monks were ideal agents of conversion. The best-known figure, possibly the greatest, is St. Columba, who founded his monastery at Iona, an island of the Inner Hebrides, in 565; a famous biography of his life was written by Adamnan, abbot of Iona, within a century of his death. Columba is believed to have been influential in converting the Picts, and he did much to support the Scots king Aidan politically.

St. Aidan brought the Celtic church to Northumbria in the 630s, establishing his monastery at Lindisfarne. At the Synod of Whitby in 664, the king of Northumbria, having to decide between the Celtic and the Roman styles of Christianity, chose the Roman version. There had been differences over such observances as the dating of Easter, but no one regarded the Celtic monks as schismatics. The Ecclesiastical History of the English People by Bede the Venerable (died 735), a monk of Jarrow in Northumbria, is a first-rate source for the early Anglo-Saxon history and shows remarkable sympathy with the Celtic clergy, though Bede was a Roman monk.

In the early 8th century the church among the Picts and Scots accepted Roman usages on such questions as Easter. Nevertheless, the church in Scotland remained Celtic in many ways until the 11th century. Still dominated by its communities of clergy (who were called Célidé or Culdees), it clearly corresponded well to the tribal nature of society.

The Norse influence

Viking raids on the coasts of Britain began at the end of the 8th century, Lindisfarne and Iona being pillaged in the 790s. By the mid-9th century Norse settlement of the western and northern isles and of Caithness and Sutherland had begun, probably largely because of overpopulation on the west coast of Norway. During the 10th century Orkney and Shetland were ruled by Norse earls nominally subject to Norway. In 1098 Magnus III (Magnus Barefoot), king of Norway, successfully asserted his authority in the northern and western isles and made an agreement with the king of Scots on their respective spheres of influence. A mid-12th-century earl of Orkney, Ragnvald, built the great cathedral at Kirkwall in honour of his martyred uncle St. Magnus.

The Norse legacy to Scotland was long-lasting, but in the mid-12th century there was a rising against the Norse in the west under a native leader, Somerled, who drove them from the greater part of mainland

Argyll. A Norwegian expedition of 1263 under King Haakon IV failed to maintain the Norse presence in the Hebrides, and three years later they were ceded to Scotland by the Treaty of Perth. In 1468–69 the northern isles of Orkney and Shetland were pawned to Scotland as part of a marriage settlement with the crown of Denmark-Norway. Nonetheless, a Scandinavian language, the Norn, was spoken in these Viking possessions, and some Norse linguistic influence still remains discernible in Shetland.

The unification of the kingdom

In 843 Kenneth MacAlpin, King Kenneth I of Scots, also became king of the Picts and crushed resistance to his assuming the throne. Kenneth may have had a claim on the Pictish throne through the matrilineal law of succession; probably the Picts too had been weakened by Norse attacks. The Norse threat helped to weld together the new kingdom of Alba and to cause its heartlands to be located in eastern Scotland, the former Pictland, with Dunkeld becoming its religious capital. But within Alba it was the Scots who established a cultural and linguistic supremacy, no doubt merely confirming a tendency seen before 843.

As the English kingdom was consolidated, its kings, in the face of Norse attacks, found it useful to have an understanding with Alba. In 945 Edmund I of England is said to have leased to Malcolm I of Alba the whole of Cumbria, probably an area including land on both sides of the western half of the later Anglo-Scottish border. In the late 10th century a similar arrangement seems to have been made for Lothian, the corresponding territory to the east. The Scots confirmed their hold on Lothian, from the Forth to the Tweed, when, about 1016, Malcolm II defeated a Northumbrian army at Carham.

About the same time, Malcolm II placed his grandson Duncan I upon the throne of the British kingdom of Strathclyde. Duncan succeeded Malcolm in 1034 and brought Strathclyde into the kingdom of Scots. During the next two centuries the Scots kings pushed their effective power north and west William I was successful in the north and Alexander II in the west until mainland Scotland became one political unit. Less discernible but as important was the way the various peoples grew together, though significant linguistic and other differences remained.

According to the Celtic system of succession, known as tanistry, a king could be succeeded by any male member of the derbfine, a family group of four generations; members of collateral branches seem to have been preferred to descendants, and the successor, or tanist, might be named in his predecessor's lifetime. This system in practice led to many successions by the killing of one's predecessor.

Thus, Duncan I was killed by his cousin Macbeth in 1040, and Macbeth was killed by Malcolm Canmore (Duncan's son, later Malcolm III Canmore) in 1057. Shakespeare freely adapted the story of Macbeth, who historically seems to have been a successful king and who may have gone on pilgrimage to Rome.

Until the 11th century the unification was the work of a Gaelic-speaking dynasty, and there is place-name evidence of the penetration of Gaelic south of the Forth. Afterward, however, the Teutonic English speech that had come to Scotland from the kingdom of Northumbria began to attain mastery, and Gaelic began its slow retreat north and west. This is not obscured by the fact that from the 12th century onward Anglo-Norman was for a time the speech of the leaders of society in England and Scotland alike. By the later Middle Ages the language known to modern scholars as Old English had evolved into two separate languages, now called Middle English and Middle Scots, with the latter focused on the court of the Stewart (Stuart) kings of Scots. After 1603 the increasing political and cultural assimilation of Scotland by England checked the further development of Scots as a separate language.

The persistence of distinctively Celtic institutions in post-12th-century Scotland is a more complex question, as will be seen from the way in which primogeniture replaced tanistry as the system of royal succession. It can be argued, however, that a Celtic stress on the family bond in society persisted throughout the Middle Ages and beyond and not only in the Highlands, with its clan organization of society.

The development of the monarchy

Malcolm Canmore came to the throne as Malcolm III in 1058 by disposing of his rivals and thereafter sought, in five unsuccessful raids, to extend his kingdom into northern England. Whereas his first wife, Ingibjorg, was the daughter of a Norse earl of Orkney, his second, Margaret, came from the Saxon royal house of England. With Margaret and her sons, Scotland was particularly receptive to cultural influence from the south. Margaret was a great patroness of the church but without altering its organization, as her sons were to do.

On the death of Malcolm III on his last English raid in 1093, sustained attempts were made to prevent the application of the southern custom of succession by primogeniture. Both Malcolm's brother and Malcolm's son by his first marriage held the throne for short periods, but it was the three sons of Malcolm and Margaret who eventually established themselves Edgar (1097–1107), Alexander I (1107–24), and David I (1124–53). Such was the force of Celtic reaction against southern influence that Edgar and Alexander could be said to have owed their thrones solely to English aid, and they were feudally subject to the English king.

The descendants of Malcolm III's first marriage continued to trouble the ruling dynasty until the early 13th century, but the descendants of his second retained the throne. Until the late 13th century the heir to the throne by primogeniture was always the obvious candidate. It is noteworthy that in charters of about 1145 David's son Henry (who was to die before his father) is described as rex designatus, very much like the tanist of the Celtic system. It is thus very hard to date precisely the acceptance of southern custom as exemplified by primogeniture.

David I (1124–53)

David I was by marriage a leading landowner in England and was well known at the English court. He was nevertheless an independent monarch, making Scotland strong by drawing on English cultural and organizational influences. Under him and his successors many Anglo-Norman families came to

Scotland, and their members were rewarded with lands and offices. Among the most important were the Bruces in Annandale, the de Morvilles in Ayrshire and Lauderdale, and the Fitzalans, who became hereditary high stewards and who, as the Stewart dynasty, were to inherit the throne in Renfrewshire. (After the 16th century the Stewart dynasty was known by its French spelling, Stuart.) Such men were often given large estates in outlying areas to bolster the king's authority where it was weak.

The decentralized form of government and society that resulted was one of the many variants of what is known as feudalism, with tenants in chief holding lands from the king and having jurisdiction over their inhabitants in return for the performance of military and other services. An essentially new element in Scottish society was the written charter, setting out the rights and obligations involved in landholding. But the way in which the Anglo-Norman families, in their position as tenants in chief, were successfully grafted onto the existing society suggests that the Celtic and feudal social systems were by no means mutually incompatible, though one stressed family bonds and the other legal contracts. The clan system of Highland Scotland became tinged with feudal influences, whereas Lowland Scottish feudalism retained a strong emphasis on the family.

David began to spread direct royal influence through the kingdom by the creation of the office of sheriff (vicecomes), a royal judge and administrator ruling an area of the kingdom from one of the royal castles. Centrally, a nucleus of government officials, such as the chancellor, the chamberlain, and the justiciar, was created by David and his successors; these officials, with other tenants in chief called to give advice, made up the royal court (Curia Regis).

This body became formalized in various ways; by the mid-13th century it might have been meeting as the king's council to discuss various types of business, and before the Wars of Independence (see below) the royal court in its capacity as the Supreme Court of Law was already being described as a Parliament. The almost total loss of all the Scottish governmental records from before the early 14th century should not lead one to underestimate the efficiency of the Scottish kings' government in this period. Historians have done much to assemble the surviving royal documents from scattered sources.

Medieval economy and society

From David's time onward the burghs, or incorporated towns, were created as centres of trade and small-scale manufacture in an overwhelmingly agrarian economy. At first all burghs probably had equal rights. Later, however, royal burghs had, by their charters, the exclusive right of overseas trade, though tenants in chief could create burghs with local trade privileges. Burghs evolved their own law to govern trading transactions, and disputes could be referred to the Court of the Four Burghs (originally Berwick, Edinburgh, Roxburgh, and Stirling).

Many of the original townspeople, or burgesses, were newcomers to Scotland. At Berwick the great trading town of the 13th century, exporting the wool of the border monasteries Flemish merchants had their own Red Hall, which they defended to the death against English attack in 1296. Besides commercial contacts with England, there is evidence of Scottish trading with the Low Countries and with Norway in the period before the Wars of Independence.

The church was decisively remodeled by David I and his successors. A clear division emerged between secular and regular clergy according to the normal western

European pattern. A complete system of parishes and dioceses was established. But the system of "appropriating" the revenue of parish churches to central religious institutions meant that the top-heaviness in wealth and resources of the church in Scotland was a built-in feature of its existence until the Reformation. Kings and other great men vied in setting up monasteries. Alexander I had founded houses of Augustinian canons at Scone and Inchcolm, while among David's foundations were the Cistercian houses of Melrose and Newbattle and the Augustinian houses of Cambuskenneth and Holyrood. Augustinian canons might also serve as the clergy of a cathedral, as they did at St. Andrews. Prominent foundations by the magnates included Walter Fitzalan's Cluniac house at Paisley and Hugh de Morville's Premonstratensian house at Dryburgh. Later royal foundations included the Benedictine house at Arbroath, established by William I.

From the standpoint of a later age, when the monasteries had lost their spiritual force, the piety of David I especially seemed a misapplication of royal resources. But the original monasteries, with their supply of trained manpower for royal service, their hospitality, and their learning, epitomized the stability that it was royal policy to achieve.

From at least 1072 the English church, particularly the archbishop of York, sought some control over the Scottish church; in the face of such a threat, the Scottish church was weakened through having no metropolitan see. But, probably in 1192, the papal bull Cum universi declared the Scottish church to be subject only to Rome, and in 1225 the bull Quidam vestrum permitted the Scottish church, lacking a metropolitan see, to hold provincial councils by authority of Rome. However, such councils, which might have served to check abuses, were seldom held.

It has been argued that the cultural developments encouraged by the church in pre-Reformation Scotland were not as great as might be expected, but this may be a false impression created because the manuscript evidence has failed to survive. The monasteries of Melrose and Holyrood each had a chronicle, and Adam of Dryburgh was an able theologian of the late 12th century. Surviving Romanesque churches show that Scotland partook of the common European architectural tradition of the time; good small examples are at Dalmeny, near Edinburgh, and at Leuchars, in Fife. Glasgow and Elgin cathedrals are noteworthy, and St. Andrews Cathedral is impressive even in its ruined state. There are also distinguished examples of castle architecture, such as Bothwell in Lanarkshire, and the castles of Argyll may reflect a distinctive mixture of influences, including Norse ones.

David I's successors

Malcolm IV (1153–65) was a fairly successful king, defeating Somerled when the latter, who had been triumphant over the Scandinavians in Argyll, turned against the kingdom of Scots. Malcolm's brother, William I ("the Lion"; 1165–1214), subdued much of the north and established royal castles there. After his capture on a raid into England, he was forced to become feudally subject to the English king by the Treaty of Falaise (1174); he was able, however, to buy back his kingdom's independence by the Quitclaim of Canterbury (1189), though it should be emphasized that this document disposed of the Treaty of Falaise and not of the less-precise claims of superiority over Scotland that English kings had put forward over the previous century. William's son, Alexander II (1214–49), subdued Argyll and was about to proceed against the Hebrides at the time of his death. His son, Alexander III (1249–86), brought the Hebrides within the Scottish kingdom in 1266, adroitly fended off

English claims to overlordship, and brought to Scotland the peace and prosperity typified by the commercial growth of Berwick. In the perspective of the subsequent Wars of Independence, it was inevitable that Scots should look back on his reign as a golden age.

The Wars of Independence

Competition for the throne

With the deaths of Alexander III in 1286 and his young granddaughter Margaret, the "Maid of Norway," four years later, almost two centuries of relatively amicable Anglo-Scottish relations came to an end. A complete uncertainty as to the proper succession to the throne provided Edward I of England and his successors with a chance to intervene in and then to assimilate Scotland. Although the two countries were feudal monarchies of a largely similar type, the English attempt was, in practice, too tactless to have any hope of success.

Besides, the struggle for independence disclosed that a marked degree of national unity had arisen among the different peoples of Scotland. Through the Anglo-Scottish conflict, Scotland developed a basic tendency to seek self-sufficiency and also to look to continental Europe for alliances and inspiration that persisted at least until 1560.

Before the death of the Maid of Norway, the Scottish interim government of "guardians" had agreed, by the Treaty of Birgham (1290), that she should marry the heir of Edward I of England, though Scotland was to be preserved as a separate kingdom. After her death 13 claimants for the Scottish crown emerged, most of them Scottish magnates. The Scots initially had no reason to suspect the motives of Edward I in undertaking to judge the various claims.

It emerged, however, that Edward saw himself not as an outside arbitrator but as the feudal superior of the

Scottish monarch and therefore able to dispose of Scotland as a fief. That Edward's interpretation was disingenuous is suggested by the fact that he had not invoked the old and vague English claims to superiority over Scotland while the Maid of Norway was still alive and he had made a treaty with Scotland on the basis of equality, not as a feudal superior claiming rights of wardship and marriage over the Maid.

The claimants to the throne, who had much to lose by antagonizing Edward, generally agreed to acknowledge his superior lordship over Scotland. But a different answer to his claim to lordship was given by the "community of the realm" (the important laymen and churchmen of Scotland as a group), who declined to commit whoever was to be king of Scots on this issue and thus displayed a sophisticated sense of national unity.

The sixth Robert de Bruce and John Balliol (see John), descendants of a younger brother of Malcolm IV and William, emerged as the leading competitors, and in 1292 Edward I named Balliol king. When Edward sought to exert his overlordship by taking law cases on appeal from Scotland and by summoning Balliol to do military service for him in France, the Scots determined to resist. In 1295 they concluded an alliance with France, and in 1296 Edward's army marched north, sacking Berwick on its way.

Edward easily forced Balliol and Scotland to submit. National resistance to English governance of Scotland grew slowly thereafter and was led by William Wallace, a knight's son, in the absence of a leader from the magnates. Wallace defeated the English at Stirling Bridge in 1297 but lost at Falkirk the next year. He was executed in London in 1305, having shown that heroic leadership without social status was not enough. When the eighth Robert de Bruce, grandson of the competitor, rose in revolt in 1306 and had himself crowned Robert I, he supplied the focus necessary to mobilize the considerable potential of national resistance.

Robert I (1306–29)

In several years of mixed fortunes thereafter, Robert the Bruce had both the English and his opponents within Scotland to contend with. Edward I's death in 1307 and the dissension in England under Edward II were assets that Robert took full advantage of. He excelled as a statesman and as a military leader specializing in harrying tactics; it is ironic that he should be remembered best for the atypical set-piece battle that he incurred and won at Bannockburn in 1314. The Declaration of Arbroath of 1320 is perhaps more informative about his methods. Ostensibly a letter from the magnates of Scotland to the pope, pledging their support for King Robert, it seems in reality to have been framed by Bernard de Linton, Robert's chancellor. In committing Robert to seeing the independence struggle through, it likewise committed those who set their seals to it. Some of them were waverers in the national cause, whether or not Robert had proof of this at the time, and his hand was now strengthened against them.

In 1328 Robert secured from England, through the Treaty of Northampton, a recognition of Scotland's independence; the following year the pope granted to the independent kings of Scots the right to be anointed with holy oil. However, Robert also died in 1329. By the appropriate standards of medieval kingship, his success had been total, but, because of the nature of medieval kingship, his successor was left with the same struggle to wage all over again.

David II (1329–71)

Robert I's son, David II, has perhaps received unfair treatment from historians contrasting him and his illustrious father. Just over five years of age at his accession, he was soon confronted with a renewal of the Anglo-Scottish war, exacerbated by the ambitions of those Scots who had been deprived of their property by Robert I or otherwise disaffected. In the 1330s Edward Balliol, pursuing the claim to the throne of his father, John, overran southern Scotland. In return for English help, he gave England southern lands and strongpoints not recaptured fully by the Scots for a century. After the Scottish defeat at Halidon Hill near Berwick in 1333, David was forced to flee to France in the following year. Berwick itself fell to the English and was never again in Scottish hands except in the period between 1461 and 1482.

The Scots gradually regained the initiative, and in 1341 David was able to return to Scotland. In 1346, however, he was captured at the Battle of Neville's

Cross near Durham. He was released in 1357 for a ransom of 100,000 merks, to be paid in nine annual installments. This ransom, three-fourths of which was eventually paid, constituted a serious burden on Scotland, and there is evidence that Parliament used this national emergency to establish some checks on the actions of the crown. In addition, the representatives of the royal burghs, which were important as an accessible source of finance, established a continuing right to sit in Parliament with the magnates and churchmen from the 1360s on, thus constituting the third of the "Three Estates."

Complex evidence relating to these transactions has been uniformly interpreted in a way discreditable to David, though another interpretation is possible. That he collected revenues more assiduously than he made ransom payments may indicate a reasoned attempt to strengthen the crown financially; and his negotiations, especially of 1363, whereby a member of the English royal house was to succeed him on the Scottish throne, may have been a diplomatic charade. Whatever his faults, David left Scotland with both its economy and its independence intact.

The long wars with England necessarily took their toll, retarding Scotland's economy and weakening the authority of its government. The buildings that have survived from this era are inferior to earlier work, much of which of course suffered damage during the wars. War was increasingly expensive, and taxation was increased drastically to pay David II's ransom. But, again, a rosier picture can be painted, suggesting that the burgesses were able to meet the increased taxation because of increased prosperity through the still-continuing trade with England.

Scotland in the 15th century
The early Stewart kings

David was succeeded by Robert II (1371–90), previously the high steward, who was the son of Robert I's daughter Marjory. The next king was Robert II's son John, restyled Robert III (1390–1406). It may be that the future Robert II's conduct was responsible for dissension in Scotland during David II's reign, particularly during his captivity in England. At any rate, neither Robert II nor his son Robert III was a strong king, and some nobles regarded both as upstarts and the latter as of doubtful legitimacy. A long period of monarchical weakness ensued in Scotland, accentuated by a series of royal minorities in the 15th and 16th centuries. Although historians have made much of the turbulence of these times, there were comparable periods of governmental weakness in contemporary England and France, and "bonds of manrent" and other alliances made by the magnates with each other and with their social inferiors should be seen as much as attempts to secure political stability in their own localities as threats to the overall peace of the kingdom.

Robert III's younger brother, Robert Stewart, 1st duke of Albany, was given powers to rule in his brother's name several times, and Robert's son James may have been sent to France in 1406 in order to keep him out of Albany's clutches. However, James was captured at sea by the English, and shortly afterward Robert III died. Following Albany's death in 1420, his son Murdac continued to misgovern the realm until 1424, when James I, then age 29, was ransomed.

The Douglas family was becoming particularly powerful in Scotland. They had been rewarded with the gift of the royal forest of Selkirk and other lands in south and southwest Scotland for loyal service to Robert I. But the growing power of the Douglases in this vital border area posed a growing threat to the crown by the end of the 14th century. At the same time, the Lords of the

Isles had attained a stature in the western Highlands that outstripped that of the kings of Scots.

One notable event was the founding of the University of Saint Andrews, Scotland's first university, in 1411. The Wars of Independence led Scottish students to go to Paris rather than to Oxford or Cambridge. But universities were the training grounds of the clergy, and when, in the period 1408–18, Scotland recognized the antipope Benedict XIII after he had been abandoned by France, it became expedient for Scotland to have its own university. The bulls of foundation from Benedict XIII reached St. Andrews in 1414.

James I (1406–37) was an active and able king, keen to once again make the crown wealthy and powerful. Perhaps he was too eager to make up for time lost in his captivity, and thus he prompted the opposition that led to his death. The new posts of comptroller and treasurer were created to gather royal revenues more efficiently. Murdac, 2nd duke of Albany, was executed in 1425, and other powerful men were overawed, even in the far north. The laws were to be revised, and in 1426 a court for civil cases was set up, presaging the later Court of Session.

In 1426, possibly to balance the power of the magnates, it was enacted that all tenants in chief should attend Parliament in person. More realistically, they were, from 1428, permitted to send representatives from each shire. Even this system did not operate until the late 16th century. If James had been inspired during his captivity by the English House of Commons, he was unable to transplant that institution to Scotland. The Scottish Parliament, like that of many other European countries, remained throughout the medieval period the feudal court of the kings of Scots; lacking the distinctive development of the English Parliament, it did not differ essentially in kind from the feudal court of any great magnate. Despite, or perhaps because of, his innovative vigour, James made enemies for himself. His murder in 1437 was part of an attempt to seize the throne for Walter Stewart, earl of Atholl, but the conspirators were executed and James's young son succeeded him.

James II (1437–60) was six years old at the time of his accession. His minority was marked by struggles between the Crichton and Livingston families. During this minority and that of James III, James Kennedy, bishop of St. Andrews, played a statesmanlike part in seeking to preserve peace. James II took a violent line against overambitious subjects. In 1452 he stabbed William Douglas, 8th earl of Douglas, to death, and in 1455 James Douglas, 9th earl of Douglas, was attainted.

The main line of the Douglas family never regained its position, though a younger, or cadet, branch of the family, the earls of Angus, was important in the late 15th century. Like his father, James II sought boldly to reassert royal authority, and Scotland lost an able king when he was killed by the bursting of a cannon at the siege of Roxburgh Castle, one of the last Scottish strongpoints in English hands. Roxburgh was subsequently captured by the Scots. Among the cultural advances of the reign was the founding, in 1451 by Bishop William Turnbull, of the University of Glasgow, Scotland's second university.

James III (1460–88), James II's son, acceded at age eight. During a period in his minority he was a pawn of the Boyd family. The Treaty of Westminster-Ardtornish of 1462 showed that John, Lord of the Isles, and the exiled Douglas were prepared to try to carve Scotland into two vassal states of England for themselves. The alliance came to nothing, but the Lords of the Isles were a threat to the territorial integrity of Scotland until their final forfeiture in 1493. Nonetheless, the power vacuum left by their removal was responsible for much of the unrest in the western Highlands thereafter. It was in James III's reign that the territory of Scotland attained its fullest extent with the acquisition of Orkney and Shetland in 1468–69.

As James III came of age, his keeping of company with artists caused grave offense to the nobles he shunned. Although it has been suggested that his fine sensibility did him credit, this is probably an anachronistic view. So serious was James's lack of authority that Berwick fell in 1482 when the nobles, led by Archibald Douglas, 5th earl of Angus, chose rather than to defend the country against the English to seize their opportunity to hang some of James's favourites. In 1488 James was murdered while fleeing from a battle against his opponents at Sauchieburn, though it seems that the death of the king was not intended, and he was succeeded without trouble by his son.

15th-century society

Despite the continuing war and unrest, there is evidence of economic recovery in Scotland during this period. Castle building and the extending of monasteries and cathedrals were widespread; work was done on the royal residences at Linlithgow and Stirling. The building of collegiate churches and of fine burgh churches is additional evidence of prosperity. Both royal burghs, with their share in international trade, and baronial burghs, with their rights in their own locality, were flourishing. The craftsmen threatened to rival the merchants in the running of burgh affairs, but an act of 1469 gave the merchants the majority on the town councils, allowing self-perpetuating cliques to misapply the assets of the burghs an abuse not remedied until the 19th century. However, the general prosperity that prevailed in Scotland was accompanied by inflation, and a debasement of the coinage added to the troubles of James III's reign.

Interesting Scottish writing from the late 14th century onward, both in the vernacular and in Latin, has survived. John Barbour (1325?–95) wrote in Scots the national epic known as The Bruce, considered the first major work of Scottish literature. A Latin history of Scotland was compiled by John of Fordun and continued by Walter Bower, abbot of Inchcolm, in his Scotichronicon. Andrew of Wyntoun wrote a history of Scotland titled Orygynale Cronykil, one of the few long examples of Middle Scots writing.

Little is left of the corpus of medieval writings in Gaelic. Nonetheless, the sophistication of the western Highland stone carvings of the later Middle Ages suggests that a strong literary culture too was associated with the courts of the Lords of the Isles and other chiefs. The Book of Deer, containing the Gospels, has in its margins an 11th-century Gaelic account of Columba's foundation of the monastery of Deer in Aberdeenshire, as well as a series of notitiae, or lists of church rights, which provide clues to the nature of Celtic society. The early 16th-century The Book of the Dean of Lismore (the seat of the bishop of Argyll) contains more than 60 Gaelic poems. From the quality of the architecture that has survived from the 15th century, one can infer the existence of paintings and other objects, such as church furnishings, that have largely disappeared. An outstandingly intricate collegiate church is that at Roslin near Edinburgh, founded by Sir William Sinclair, 3rd earl of Orkney, about 1450. There are fine burgh churches, such as St. John's in Perth and the Church of the Holy Rood in Stirling. Perhaps the outstanding piece of evidence of royal patronage of the arts is the altarpiece for James III's Trinity College Church in Edinburgh, which is almost certainly the work of the great Flemish painter Hugo van der Goes.

In the 14th century the papacy had built up its claims to appoint to the higher offices in the church; in Scotland it had established a system of "provisions," or papal appointments, to vacant offices. This did not merely cut across the rights of rulers, who used the church to provide their loyal bureaucrats with a living, and the rights of other local patrons; it also meant a drain to Rome of money in the form of the tax payable by a cleric "provided" to a vacant post by the pope. James I resisted these developments, and at the same time, in the Council of Basel (1431–49), the conciliarists were seeking to curb papal power in the church; a distinguished member of the Council of Basel was the Scot Thomas Livingston, one of the first St. Andrews graduates.

James also sought to revive the monastic ideal in its early purity and established a house of the strict Carthusians at Perth. A compromise between James I and the pope was probably pending when James was murdered, and his successors tended to let the popes collect their money as long as they "provided" to church offices along lines acceptable to the monarchy. In 1487 James III was granted the concession that the pope would delay promotions to the higher offices for eight months so that the king could propose his nominee.

St. Andrews was made the seat of an archbishopric in 1472, in itself a desirable step. But the first archbishop of St. Andrews secured the honour by supporting the papacy against the king, and, as a result, the appointment was not welcomed in Scotland. Glasgow also became an archbishopric in 1492.

Scotland in the 16th and early 17th centuries

James IV (1488–1513) and James V (1513–42)

James IV, being physically impressive, cultured, generous, and active in politics and war alike, was well-equipped for kingship. In 1493 he eliminated a potential rival by carrying out the forfeiture of the last Lord of the Isles, and he also dealt severely with unrest on the English border and elsewhere. James and Bishop William Elphinstone of Aberdeen founded King's College, Scotland's third university, in Aberdeen in 1495. This was the great age of Scottish poetry, and, while one of the leading makars, or poets, Robert Henryson (1420/30?–c. 1506), author of The Testament of Cresseid, was a burgh schoolmaster, the others were members of the court circle; Gawin Douglas (1475?–1522), bishop of Dunkeld and kinsman to the earls of Angus, splendidly translated Virgil's Aeneid into Scots, and William Dunbar (1460/65–

1520), a technically brilliant poet, showed the versatility of which Scots was capable.

After initial disharmony with England, James concluded a "treaty of perpetual peace" with Henry VII in 1502 and married Margaret, Henry's daughter, in 1503. But Henry VIII of England became involved in the anti-French schemes of Pope Julius II, and in 1512 France and Scotland renewed their "auld alliance" as a counterbalance. In 1513 Henry VIII invaded France. James IV consequently invaded England, where he died along with thousands of his army in the rashly fought and calamitous Battle of Flodden.

James's efficiency at home was thus offset by his excessive international ambitions. And both had cost money for artillery, for a navy whose greatest ship, the Great Michael, cost £30,000, and for embassies. The crown granted lands in feu-farm tenure, which gave heritable possession in return for a substantial down payment and an unchangeable annual rent thereafter. In the great European inflation of the 16th century (known traditionally as the "price revolution"), this policy weakened the crown over the long term.

James V (1513–42) acceded to the throne when he was 17 months of age. The factional struggles of his minority were given shape by the division between those who adhered to Scotland's pro-French alignment and those who were determined that the price Scotland paid at Flodden not be repeated. John Stewart, 2nd duke of Albany, was regent until 1524 and favoured France; Archibald Douglas, 6th earl of Angus, maintained a pro-English policy until 1528, when James began his personal rule. James now found Scotland's support in international politics being sought on all sides.

In the 1530s he obtained papal financial help in establishing a College of Justice, and he concluded two successive French marriages, each bringing a substantial dowry; his second wife, Mary, daughter of the duke de Guise, became the mother of Mary, Queen of Scots. James's support for the papacy and France alienated some of his subjects, however, and his rule was not simply strict and financially vigorous but rather avaricious and vindictive. Lack of noble support seems to have caused the rout at Solway Moss in November 1542 of a force invading England. This and the deaths of his infant sons led to the death of James, probably from nervous prostration, in December, a week after the birth of his daughter, Mary.

Mary (1542–67) and the Scottish Reformation

The church in 16th-century Scotland may not have had more ignorant or immoral priests than those of previous generations, but restiveness at their shortcomings was becoming more widespread, and the power structure of the church seemed to preclude the possibility of reform without revolution. The church made a poor showing at the parish level, since by 1560 the bulk of the revenues of nearly 9 parishes in every 10 was appropriated to monasteries and other central institutions. In return for receiving its share of this wealth, the papacy abandoned spiritual direction of the Scottish church; from 1487 royal control over appointments to the higher church offices grew steadily.

That this occurred at a time when the church's annual revenue reckoned at £400,000 in 1560 was 10 times that of the crown readily explains the attraction of church office for unspiritual, career-seeking nobles. Laymen were feued (granted tenure of) church lands, became collectors of church revenues, and were given abbeys as benefices. Church property, particularly monastic property, was effectively being secularized, and if Protestantism offered to the nobles and lairds of

Scotland a more spiritually alive church and one with lay participation it probably also appealed to them as a system under which they would not have to hand back what they had grabbed.

Particular laymen were as pious as ever, endowing collegiate churches as they had once endowed monasteries, and trenchant criticism of church abuses was expressed in the morality play Ane Pleasant Satyre of the Thrie Estaitis by Sir David Lyndsay (c. 1490–c. 1555). Nonetheless, reform from within was probably almost impossible. For example, Archbishop John Hamilton, a would-be reformer who gave his name to a vernacular catechism (1552), belonged to the family who had the most to lose if the careerists were curbed.

Mary began her reign (1542–67) as another Stewart child ruler in the hands of factions. The pro-French party upheld the old church, while the pro-English desired reform. By the Treaties of Greenwich (1543),

Mary was to marry Edward, Henry VIII's heir. David Beaton, archbishop of St. Andrews and a papal legate in Scotland from 1544, and Mary of Guise, the queen mother, had this policy rescinded, and the murder of Beaton (1546) and English punitive raids culminating in the Scottish defeat at Pinkie (1547) did not cause Scotland to love England more. France helped Scotland to expel the English, but only in return for such a hold over the country that, by the time of young Mary's marriage to the dauphin in 1558, France appeared to be about to absorb Scotland.

Anti-French feeling and Protestant preaching combined to bring about revolt. In 1559 the reformers took up arms to forestall Mary of Guise's action against them. Despite the preaching of John Knox and others and the plundering of the monasteries, the decisive issues were political and military: Queen Elizabeth I of England sent troops to check French plans in Scotland. Mary of Guise died in June 1560, and, by the Treaty of Edinburgh in

July, both France and England undertook to withdraw their troops. With Scotland thus neutralized, England's proximity to Scotland gave it an important advantage over France.

In August 1560 the Scottish Parliament abolished papal authority and adopted a Reformed Confession of Faith, but Mary, still in France, did not ratify this legislation. Still, the organization of local congregations, which had been going on for some years, continued, and the General Assembly emerged as the central legislative body for the church. In the First Book of Discipline (1560), Knox and other ministers proposed a striking social program for the church that would provide education and relief for the poor. However, laymen had not despoiled the old church to enrich the new, and, as an interim settlement secured by Mary's government in 1562, the church and crown together were to share but one-third of the old church's revenue.

Mary's husband died in 1560, and in 1561 she returned to Scotland. As a Roman Catholic in a Protestant land and as nearest heir, by descent from Henry VII's daughter, to Elizabeth of England, she had many enemies. Her personal reign was brief and dramatic: she married her cousin Henry Stewart, Lord Darnley (1565); their son, James (the future James VI of Scotland and James I of England), was born (1566); Darnley was murdered (1567); Mary married the adventurer James Hepburn, 4th earl of Bothwell the instigator of Darnley's murder prompting Mary's imprisonment and forcing her abdication (1567); and Mary escaped and fled to England (1568). Her task as a ruler was hard and made more difficult by her own errors of judgment but she essayed it bravely and was a truly tragic rather than a pathetic figure.

James VI (1567–1625)

James lived through the usual disrupted minority to become one of Scotland's most successful kings. In a civil war between his own and his mother's followers, laird (landed proprietor) and merchant support for James may have been decisive in his eventual victory. Queen Elizabeth detained Mary in England and assisted James Douglas, 4th earl of Morton, regent from 1572, in achieving stability in Scotland.

James's government ratified the Reformed church settlement, and more permanent measures of church endowment were taken. The Concordat of Leith (1572) allowed the crown to appoint bishops with the church's approval. As in Mary's reign, the crown was intervening to prevent the wealth of the old church from being entirely laicized. And if the bishopric revenues were saved from going the same way as the monastic wealth, the crown expected a share in them for its services.

A new presbyterian party in the church, whose members wanted parity for all ministers and freedom from state control, rejected this compromise. Led by Andrew Melville, a rigid academic theorist, they demanded, in the Second Book of Discipline (1578), that the new church receive all the wealth of the old, that it be run by a hierarchy of courts rather than of bishops, and that the state leave the church alone but be prepared to take advice from it. Many historians have seen these demands, as James undoubtedly did, as an attempt to establish a full-blown theocracy. James was not strong enough for out-and-out resistance immediately, and he sometimes made concessions, as in the Golden Act of 1592, which gave parliamentary sanction to the system of presbyterian courts.

But he gradually showed his determination to run the church his own way, through the agency of his bishops, who were brought into Parliament in 1600. From 1606

Melville was detained in London, and he was later banished. By 1610 the civil and ecclesiastical status of the bishops was secure. The continued existence of church courts kirk sessions, presbyteries, synods, and the General Assembly shows James's readiness for compromise, and he showed a wise cautiousness toward liturgical reform after encountering hostility over his Five Articles of Perth (1618), which imposed kneeling at communion, observance of holy days, confirmation, infant baptism, and other practices.

In the 1580s, as James became personally responsible for royal policy, he faced the need to control unruly subjects at home, nobles and kirkmen alike, and to win friends abroad. He concluded a league with England in 1586, and when Elizabeth executed his mother in the following year as a Roman Catholic threat to the English throne, he acquiesced in what he could not prevent. He thus inherited his mother's claim, and his efforts thereafter to keep in the good graces of

Elizabeth and her minister William Cecil were successful. He succeeded peacefully to the English throne in 1603, though his two monarchies, despite his own personal inclinations, remained distinct from each other.

James's policy was one of overall insurance; he avoided giving offense to Catholic continental rulers, and, while he dealt effectively with lawbreakers on the border and elsewhere, he showed marked leniency toward his Catholic nobles, even when the discovery of letters and blank documents (the "Spanish Blanks" affair, 1592) showed that several of them were in treasonable conspiracy with a foreign power. Neither a heroic king, like James IV, nor the pedantic and cowardly buffoon depicted in Sir Walter Scott's The Fortunes of Nigel, James VI was a supple and able politician. His theories of divine-right monarchy were a scholar-king's response to an age when the practice and theory of regicide were fashionable. Except perhaps at the very end of his life, James was too realistic to let his theories entirely govern his conduct.

James excelled in picking good servants from among the lairds and burgesses; they were his judges and privy councillors and sat on the Committee of Articles, with which he dominated Parliament. After 1603 they governed Scotland smoothly in his absence. From 1587 Parliament was made more representative by the admission of shire commissioners to speak for the lairds, and the program of James I was thus realized. The privy council had judicial as well as legislative and administrative functions; there were, in addition, the Court of Session for civil cases (it had evolved from the council in the early 16th century and, as the College of Justice, had been endowed with church funds in the 1530s) and justice courts for criminal cases. Local justice and administration continued, however, despite James VI's efforts, to be largely the prerogative of the landowners.

Scotland still had a subsistence economy, exporting raw materials and importing finished goods, including luxuries. However, the luxury imports illustrate that the greater landowners and merchants were gaining in prosperity. Despite the absence of adequate endowment, the Reformed church began to create a network of parish schools, and there were advances in the universities. Melville brought discipline and the latest scholarship to Glasgow and St. Andrews in turn, and there were new foundations at Edinburgh (the Town's College, 1582) and Aberdeen (Marischal College, 1593).

As the continual strife between England and Scotland receded, they drew closer together. Although the national churches in England and Scotland were not identical in structure, they shared a common desire to protect and preserve the Reformation. James VI's accession to the English throne in 1603 as James I encouraged further cultural and economic assimilation.

It was far from guaranteeing further political assimilation, but a century of the barely workable personal union of the crowns had increasingly sharpened the Scots' dilemma of choosing between complete union and complete separation.

The Age of Revolution (1625–89)

Charles I (1625–49)

James VI's son, Charles I, was raised in England and lacked any understanding of his Scottish subjects and their institutions. He soon fell foul of a restless nobility in a Scotland that lacked the natural focal point of a royal court. The king also caused widespread anger by high taxation, by the special demands made on Edinburgh to build a Parliament House and to provide a cathedral for the bishopric founded there in 1633, and by a Spanish war and a French war that were intended to further English diplomacy but meanwhile disrupted Scottish trading ties. The aristocratic leaders of the opposition found ideal material on which to build clerical and popular support. Charles and his Scottish bishops were fond enough of ritual and splendour in church services to make plausible the (wholly incorrect) suggestion that they were ready for compromise with Rome. The new Book of Canons (1635–36) and Liturgy (1637) therefore offended by their content, as well as by being authorized by royal prerogative alone. The National Covenant (1638) astutely collected national support for the opposition's pledge to resist Charles's innovations. Condemnation of popery was written into it for the benefit of those who feared that Charles might be a crypto-Catholic; others, more sophisticated, welcomed its implicit condemnation of a royal arbitrariness with religion and private rights that was contrary to all Scottish precedent.

The Covenanters humbled Charles in two almost bloodless campaigns, the Bishops' Wars (1639–40), leaving him with no alternative but to ask for money from an English Parliament in which his opponents were strongly represented. Charles had authorized a general assembly of the Scottish church (1638) and a Scottish Parliament (1639); the Covenanters packed these meetings, scrapped all the king's innovations, and abolished episcopacy. Thus, by 1641 there was a revolutionary situation in both kingdoms, and in August 1642 war broke out between Charles and his English opponents.

Both sides sought Scottish help, which was soon accorded to the English parliamentary opposition. By the Solemn League and Covenant (1643) the English promised, in return for military aid, to help preserve government by the Presbyterian church in Scotland and, so at least the Scots believed, to set it up in England. James Graham, 1st marquess of Montrose, and others who then left the Covenanting side argued that by this second Covenant, and by certain constitutional constraints they had placed upon the crown, the Scots had gone unwarrantably far beyond the aims of the first Covenant. But those Scots who were prepared to make common cause with the English opposition, even if the English did have a more deep-seated quarrel with their king than the Scots, had reasoned justification, for it was realistic to expect that Charles, as soon as it proved possible, would withdraw concessions made to men whom he regarded as his enemies.

Personal antipathies also helped to split the ranks of the original Covenanters notably the antipathy between Montrose and Archibald Campbell, 1st marquess of Argyll, who was sincerely devoted to the cause but equally devoted to the advancement of his family. Montrose's military efforts for Charles in Scotland were crushed in 1645, and by 1646 Charles had also lost the war in England. When Charles surrendered to the Scottish army in England, the Scots failed to reach agreement with him and handed him over to the English.

The Scottish contribution to the English war effort had been substantial but not spectacular enough to leave a sense of obligation, and the English army under Oliver Cromwell, who now eclipsed Parliament in English politics, preferred Independency to Presbyterianism in the church and did not propose to honour the Solemn League and Covenant. A conservative element among the Covenanters in 1647 reached a compromise, or "Engagement," with Charles by which they promised him help in return for the establishment of Presbyterianism in both kingdoms for three years and went to war on his behalf; their ill-planned campaign was crushed at Preston in 1648. The clerics, who had bitterly opposed this compromise, were now able, under the leadership of a few nobles such as Argyll, to purge the Scottish Parliament and army of all those tainted by collaboration with the king. The execution of

Charles by the English in 1649 genuinely shocked most Scots, who were prepared to fight for his son, Charles II, once he had been constrained to accept the Covenants and once Montrose had been executed (1650). Cromwell's victory over the Scots at Dunbar (1650) gave more-moderate Scots the ascendancy again, but this brought no better military result. Another, and decisive, defeat at Cromwell's hands came to a Scottish royalist army at Worcester in 1651.

Cromwell

Cromwell imposed on Scotland a full and incorporating parliamentary union with England (1652). However, this union, maintained by an army of occupation, did not enjoy popular consent. Nevertheless, Cromwell's administration of Scotland was efficient, and his judges, some of them Englishmen, achieved an admired impartiality. Public order was well maintained, even in the Highlands after the collapse of royalist resistance in 1654. Cromwell did not overturn Presbyterianism but ensured toleration for others, save Roman Catholics and Episcopalians (those who believed the Protestant church should be governed by bishops).

The Restoration monarchy

The restoration in 1660 of Charles II (1660–85) was welcomed by many moderates in both Scotland and England. Charles had learned much from his father's fate and was prepared to forget many injuries, though his government executed some Scots, including the marquess of Argyll.

In 1662 Charles formally restored church government by bishops, but, like the compromise fashioned under James VI, they were to act in association with synods and presbyteries. Charles seems to have been moved not by rancor toward the Covenanters, who had bullied him in the early 1650s, but merely by a desire to achieve the system that satisfied most people. Many laymen accepted his system, and few nobles opposed it. However, approximately 270 ministers just over a quarter of the total were deprived of their parishes for noncompliance, leading to the Pentland Rising (1666), which was easily quashed and was countered by an experimental period of tolerance by the government.

Persons who still persisted in attending conventicles were strong only in the southwest and to some extent in Fife and among the small lairds and common people. These men adhered to the "Protester" position, regarding Scotland as still bound by the Covenants. In another trial of strength with the government, they were defeated at Bothwell Bridge (1679). Some Cameronians (the name derives from Richard Cameron, a leading Covenanter) remained, meeting governmental violence with further violence, and in 1690 they refused to join a Presbyterian but uncovenanted Church of Scotland. Their brave and fanatic "thrawnness" (recalcitrance) endeared them to later generations of Scots.

When Charles's brother succeeded as James VII of Scotland and James II of Great Britain and Ireland (1685–88), most Scots showed that they were prepared to support him despite his Roman Catholicism. But he showed his ineptitude by requesting Parliament to grant toleration to Catholics (1686); this stirred up unprecedented opposition to royal wishes in the Scottish Parliament. Nevertheless, although many exiled Scots were at the court of William of Orange in Holland, the collapse (1688–89) of James's regime in Scotland was entirely a result of the Glorious Revolution (1688) in England and the landing there of William.

The era of union
The revolution settlement

With James VII having fled to France, a Convention of Estates (really the same assembly as Parliament but meeting less formally) gave the crown jointly to the Protestant William of Orange (William III of Great Britain, 1689–1702) and his wife, Mary II (1689–94), James's daughter. William's first major decision was a moderate one: episcopacy was abolished in 1689 and Presbyterianism reestablished the following year. However, a series of crises throughout William's reign exposed his total lack of interest in Scotland and placed a strain on the system that had developed whereby the Scottish ministry took orders not only from the monarch but also from the English ministry.

The Act of Union and its results

William fought one war against France (1689–97) and on his death in 1702 bequeathed another (1701–13) to his successor, his wife's sister Anne (1702–14). These circumstances made a union of Scotland and England seem strategically as well as economically desirable. That an Act of Union was achieved in 1707 is at first sight surprising, since intervening sessions of the Scottish Parliament had been in a mood to break the English connection altogether. But by 1707 England's appreciation of its own strategic interests, and of the nuisance value of the Scottish Parliament, was lively enough for it to offer statesmanlike concessions to Scotland and material inducements to Scottish parliamentarians to accept union.

The union was an incorporating one the Scottish Parliament was ended and the Westminster Parliament increased by 45 commoners and 16 peers representing Scotland. Scotland benefited by gaining free trade with England and its colonies, by the grant of a money "equivalent" of the share of the English national debt that Scotland would assume, and by the explicit safeguarding of its national church and legal system. After Queen Anne's death in 1714, when the Jacobites, supporters of James VII's descendants, missed their best opportunity, the worst crises of the union were past.

Jacobitism in the Highlands

The Jacobites were seldom more than a nuisance in Britain. An expedition from France in 1708 and a West Highland rising with aid from Spain in 1719 were abortive; bad leadership in the rebellion in 1715 (known as "the Fifteen Rebellion") of James VII's son, James Edward, the Old Pretender, and divided counsels in the rebellion of 1745 ("the Forty-five") led by the Old Pretender's son Charles Edward, the Young Pretender, crippled invasions originating in France that had in any case less than an even chance of success. The government was not always sufficiently prepared for invasions, but the generalship of John Campbell, 2nd duke of Argyll, at Sheriffmuir in 1715 sufficed to check the Jacobites, and that of William Augustus, duke of

Cumberland, at Culloden in 1746 dealt the coup de grâce to a Jacobite army.

The Jacobites never had full French naval and military assistance, and support in Scotland itself was limited; not many more Lowland Scots than Englishmen loved the Stuarts enough to die for them. Many politicians, especially before 1714, corresponded with the royal exiles simply as a matter of insurance against their return, and in the dying days of Stuart hopes there were fewer people than there have been since who were struck by the romantic aura surrounding Prince Charles Edward, "Bonnie Prince Charlie." The Stuarts primarily had to rely on the clans of the Gaelic-speaking regions, and Highland support in itself alienated Lowlanders.

Not all Highlanders were "out" in the Fifteen or the Forty-five rebellions; such clans as the Campbells and the Munros, the Macleods, and the Macdonalds of

Sleat were Hanoverian either because they were Presbyterian or through their chiefs' personal inclinations. However, many clans were Roman Catholic or Episcopalian and favoured a Catholic monarch; they were legitimists and reasonably so, since both James VII and his son, James Edward, the Old Pretender, appreciated Highland problems problems of an infertile land overpopulated with fighting men who owed personal allegiance to their chiefs and who were partly dependent on plunder to maintain their standard of living.

The years after the Battle of Culloden were characterized by a series of attempts by the chiefs in the late 18th and particularly in the early 19th century to emulate the new capitalist agriculture of the Lowlands, thus creating an impersonal cash relationship with their tenants based on the exploitative employment of the latter in industries such as the harvesting of kelp (seaweed) for its alkali content or stimulating recruiting to newly formed regiments of the British army. The roots of this process can be found prior to the defeat of Jacobitism, but the catastrophe of the Fifteen and Forty-five rebellions made the process more rapid and more painful. The atrocities of government soldiers and the repressiveness of government legislation after 1746 were much less important in ushering in the new order than economic and social forces.

The Scottish Enlightenment

No straightforward connection can be drawn between the union and the exceptional 18th-century flowering of intellectual life known as the Scottish Enlightenment. Absence of civil strife, however, permitted the best minds to turn, if they chose, from politics and its 17th-century twin, religion, and few of the best minds from 1707 onward were in fact directly concerned with politics. Philosophy, in which 18th-century Scotland excelled, was a proper concern for a country where for generations minds had been sharpened by theological debate. Scottish culture remained distinctive, and distinctively European in orientation.

The historian and philosopher David Hume sought to remove Scotticisms from his speech, and the architect Robert Adam gained extra experience as well as income from being able to design buildings in London as well as in Edinburgh. Nevertheless, Adam drew most of his stylistic inspiration from the Classical architecture he had studied in Italy, and Hume, "le bon David," was an honoured member of Continental polite and intellectual society. Hume's The History of England (1754–62) made his literary reputation in his lifetime, but it is his philosophical works, such as his A Treatise of Human Nature (1739–40), that have caused the continuous growth of his reputation since his death. Adam Smith, author of The Wealth of Nations (1776), was the philosopher of political economy.

The discipline of history was developed by William Robertson, a Church of Scotland clergyman, principal of the University of Edinburgh, and official historiographer royal for Scotland; his History of Scotland, During the Reigns of Queen Mary and of King James VI was published in 1759. Henry Home, Lord Kames, may be singled out from a number of other significant figures to illustrate the versatility characteristic of the times.

He was a judge, interested in legal theory and history, an agricultural reformer in theory and practice, a commissioner of the Forfeited Estates (of the rebels of 1745), and a member of the Board of Trustees for Manufactures (which encouraged Scottish industries, notably linen production). In poetry there was a reaction, possibly against union and certainly against assimilation with England; revived interest in Scots vernacular poetry of the past was the herald of a spate of new vernacular poetry, which culminated in the satires of Robert Fergusson and the lyrics of Robert Burns. Some of the greatest Gaelic poets, such as Alexander MacDonald, were also writing at this time.

The Scottish educational system, its foundations so securely laid throughout the previous century, made possible this extraordinary cultural outpouring. The Scottish universities enjoyed their heyday, Edinburgh being notable for medicine and preeminent in most other subjects as well. Gradually the regents, who taught students throughout their university course, were replaced by professors specializing in single subjects.

That students seldom troubled to graduate was of little disadvantage in an age when appointments depended on patronage. Not bound by a rigid curriculum, students were able to indulge the Scots' traditionally wide intellectual curiosity by attending lectures in a variety of subjects. Scientific study was encouraged, and practical applications of discoveries were given due place. Francis Home, professor of Materia Medica at Edinburgh, studied bleaching processes and plant nutrition; and James Watt, instrument maker to the University of Glasgow for a time, was encouraged by the university to work on the steam engine, to which he was to make crucial improvements.

19th-century Scotland

Agitation for constitutional change was considered treasonable by many during the years 1793–1815, when Britain was fighting Revolutionary France. Several advocates of universal suffrage, including a young Glasgow lawyer, Thomas Muir of Huntershill, were sentenced to transportation (exile) in 1793. After repression had broken this first radical wave, postwar industrial depression produced another the "Radical War" of 1820, an abortive rising of workers in the

Glasgow area. Intellectual campaigning of a more moderate sort had greater short-term success.

The Edinburgh Review, founded in 1802 by a group of young lawyers led by Francis Jeffrey and Henry Brougham (1st Baron Brougham and Vaux), was influential in both radical politics and literature. Edinburgh life was particularly brilliant during the war years, when students unable to study abroad found the University of Edinburgh more attractive than ever. Outstanding in this period was Sir Walter Scott, although not until 1827 was he known to be the author of the Waverley novels. Scott's greatness as a novelist lay in the way he took Scottish society as a whole for his main character, and his best books are a lament for an era that he knew was dying, the organic society of preindustrial Scotland.

The other major figure in 19th-century Scottish fiction was Robert Louis Stevenson, who published a wide variety of historical novels, adventure stories, and travel literature before his premature death in Samoa in 1894. His voice, especially from exile, was distinctive. Scottish writing in the 1890s is generally perceived to be sentimental and mawkish, exemplified by the Kailyard novels of Sir James Barrie, Samuel Rutherford Crockett, and Ian Maclaren; George Douglas perhaps overcompensated for this tendency in The House with the Green Shutters (1901), the first realistic portrayal of Scottish life. Gaelic poetry is generally held to have been in decline for much of the 19th century until the work of Iain Mac a'Ghobhainn (John Smith), Uilleam MacDhunlèibhe (William Livingstone), and the political activist Màiri Mhór nan Oran (Mary Macpherson) in the final third of the century.

The Industrial Revolution

From the 1820s the Industrial Revolution was in full swing in Scotland, linked (in a way historians have not altogether disentangled) to a dramatic increase in population. There were perhaps a million people in Scotland at the beginning of the 18th century. By the beginning of the 19th century there were more than 1.5 million, and by the turn of the 20th century the population exceeded 4.5 million. The manufacturing towns showed spectacular increases. Hundreds of thousands of Irish emigrants went to Scotland in the 19th century, beginning prior to but increasing in number during the Irish Potato Famine of 1845–49.

In some country regions there was a population decrease as people moved to the towns, to England, or overseas. Part of the overall increase was the result of improved medical care that had lessened the ravages of epidemic diseases by the mid-19th century. Much of the food for the increased population was supplied by progressive Scottish agriculture. Farming in the southeast was celebrated for its efficiency in the early

19th century, and the northeast became famous for its beef cattle and Ayrshire for its milking herds.

The key advance was in heavy industry, which from about 1830 took the industrial primacy from textiles, at a time when industry as a whole had replaced agriculture as Scotland's chief concern. Coal production rose, as did that of iron, with the hot-blast process (1828) of James Beaumont Neilson making Scottish ores cheaper to work. Major canals, such as the Forth and Clyde, completed in 1790, enjoyed a short boom before being rendered obsolete by the railways, of which the Glasgow-to-Garnkirk (1831) was noteworthy for using steam locomotives (rather than horses) from its inception. Above all, Scottish international trade was catered to, and Clydeside's reputation made, by the building of ships. Robert Napier was the greatest of many great Scottish marine engineers. The later 19th century was characterized by the expansion of new heavy industry, such as steel, and technological advances in shipbuilding and marine engineering.

Politics and religion

Parliamentary (1832) and burgh (1833) reform ended fictitious county votes and corrupt burgh caucuses but disillusioned the working classes by failing to extend to them the franchise. As in England, they had to await the 1867 and subsequent Reform Acts (see Reform Bill). But the great bulk of the Scottish middle classes were delighted with the Whigs, who had brought the reforms. The Whig Party, or Liberal Party (as it became known in the 1860s), dominated Scottish mid-19th-century politics. Liberal Party leader and hero William Ewart Gladstone, of Scottish parentage, was widely admired among Scots for his moral dynamism and fire despite his High Church Episcopalianism.

Ecclesiastical strife was perhaps more important than parliamentary politics in Scottish life in the 19th century. Opposing approaches to the relationship between church and state within the Church of Scotland brought about the Ten Years' Conflict, which was not resolved until a large proportion of the clergy and the laity left the established Church of Scotland in 1843 to form the Free Church of Scotland. This fracture was not healed until the Presbyterian reunion in 1929, and it had profound effects on Scottish life, because the church was the main agency of social welfare (until 1845) under the old Poor Law of Scotland and undertook a similar role in the Scottish education system until 1872.

Trade unions of skilled workers had led an uninterrupted existence since the early 19th century. By the 1880s unskilled workers were being organized. Various factors delayed the permanent organization of the miners until a major leader, James Keir Hardie, emerged from their ranks. Failing to sufficiently engage the Liberals in support of organized labour, he helped form the Scottish Labour Party in 1888. In 1893 Hardie created the Independent Labour Party (ILP) for Britain as a whole, and in 1900 the ILP federated with the trade unions for the purpose of running the Labour Party (given its present name in 1906). However, liberalism continued to dominate Scottish politics until 1922 (the Liberals even won a majority of Scottish seats in the two general elections of 1910), as the labour movement, despite the activity of Hardie, found it difficult to emerge from the shadow of the Liberals.

The Highlands

By 1800 the Highlands had become overpopulated relative to the means of subsistence. Many lairds, seeking to support their tenantry through the kelp industry, were ruined when it collapsed in the period from 1815 to 1825. Other landowners introduced sheep, sometimes violently removing their tenants in the "Highland Clearances" as agents of the Sutherland family did in Strathnaver, Sutherland, about 1810–20. The Potato Famine in the Scottish Highlands that began in the mid-1840s caused distress and encouraged landowners to engage in a new round of clearances and to sponsor large-scale emigration.

By the 1880s Highland subsistence-farming tenants, or "crofters," faced a new problem. Deer forests had replaced sheep runs as the most immediately profitable land use open to landowners, and, as a result, the shortage of land for grazing and arable agriculture was the major grievance of the crofting community. Parliamentary agitation by the crofters, who voted for the first time in 1885, and by their Lowland sympathizers, as well as sporadic outbursts of violence beginning in 1882 (the "Crofters' War"), secured an act of 1886 that gave the crofters security of tenure and empowered a Crofters' Commission to fix fair rents, though it did little to make more land available to crofters. (Further legislation in 1911 and

1919 helped to alleviate this problem.) Unlike their Irish counterparts, the Highlanders sought not ownership of their land but the imposition of certain standards of conduct and responsibility upon their landlords. As the crofting agitation of the 1880s united both Highlanders and Lowlanders, it was a key stage in the forging of a modern Scottish consciousness.

Scotland since World War I

World War I and after

World War I had a great effect on Scottish society; 74,000 Scots were killed and industry mobilized as never before in a coordinated national effort. Clyde shipbuilding and engineering were crucial, and Clydeside was the key munitions centre in Britain. In retrospect, however, the expansion of heavy industry in the 1920s was in fact an overexpansion. The collapse of the wartime boom in 1920 began a period of economic depression in Britain, in which Scotland was one of the worst-affected regions.

Economic distress bred political radicalism. The Liberals were eclipsed, and in most seats the real contest was between the Unionists and Labour, which became Scotland's biggest single party for the first time in the election of 1922. Willie Gallacher, Scotland's only notable communist member of Parliament and an able political theorist strongly influenced by Vladimir Lenin, was at the same time a radical belonging to a revered Scots tradition.

In 1930 John Wheatley, who had been minister of health in the first Labour government (1924) and the author of an important housing act, died, thereby depriving left-wingers in the Labour Party of a skilled leader, and counsels of moderation in the party prevented its taking any distinctive initiative on the economic crisis. Ramsay MacDonald, a Scot who had led two minority Labour governments, agreed to form a national coalition government with Conservative and Liberal support in 1931. However, the Labour Party refused to participate, disowned MacDonald, and was heavily defeated at the polls in Scotland as elsewhere.

Another political development that resulted partly from economic distress was the formation in 1934 of the Scottish National Party (SNP), a merger of two previous parties. It had some distinguished supporters, especially literary figures, but it was suspected, sometimes unfairly, of political extremism and made little electoral impact before World War II. The national government of the 1930s was dominated by the Conservatives. While opposed to an independent Scottish legislature, this government furthered the extension of the Scottish administrative system in 1939, installing it in St. Andrew's House in Edinburgh.

The interwar period was one of significant cultural advance and self-confidence in Scotland. In poetry the dominant figure in this renaissance was Christopher Murray Grieve, who published under the pseudonym Hugh MacDiarmid. Important achievements in prose literature were made by Neil Gunn, Edwin Muir, Nan Shepherd, and Willa Muir. James Leslie Mitchell (Lewis Grassic Gibbon) published a trilogy of novels, collectively known as A Scots Quair (1932–34), which charted the changes in the social life of the communities of northeastern Scotland. In Gaelic literature poetry continued to be the dominant form, and the lyrical work of Somhairle MacGill-eain (Sorley Maclean) dominated the 20th-century scene.

World War II and after

During World War II Scotland suffered some 34,000 combat deaths, and approximately 6,000 civilians were killed, many in air attacks on Clydeside. In 1943 Tom

Johnston, a Labour member of Parliament who acted as secretary of state for Scotland in the wartime national government, helped to create the North of Scotland Hydro-Electric Board, which was one of the most successful government agencies of the period.

In 1945 Labour won a landslide national election victory that gave it 37 of Scotland's 74 seats in Parliament to the Conservatives' 32. Support for Labour gradually ebbed in the early 1950s, however, and in 1955 the Conservative Party took 36 of 71 Scottish seats, its first majority in Scotland. These gains were reversed in 1959, when the Conservatives lost 3 seats in Scotland, despite the party's net gain of 23 seats nationally.

The Scottish economy was relatively healthy from 1945 through the mid-1950s. The Labour governments (1945–51) sought to ensure full employment, and though the Conservatives initially opposed Labour's widespread nationalization of industries such as the coal mines, the Bank of England, the railroads, and electric power they eventually accepted the mixed economy and the expanded welfare state. The Scottish Milk Marketing Board helped to boost Scotland's agricultural productivity. However, Scotland's heavy industries especially coal mining and shipbuilding began to stagnate in the mid-1950s, and unemployment in Scotland was often twice that in England. In its 1961 report on the Scottish economy, the Scottish Council for Development and Industry remarked that "if there is a panacea for Scotland's economic problems we have not found it."

Scottish nationalism was relatively muted in the 1950s, despite the signing of a Scottish Covenant, which called for home rule in Scotland, reportedly by more than two million Scots in 1949, and despite the theft of the Stone of Scone, the ancient stone upon which Scottish kings were traditionally crowned, from Westminster

Abbey on Christmas Day 1950 (the stone, which was taken to Scotland, was returned in April 1951). By the late 1950s Scottish nationalists supported independence or the creation of a devolved assembly, though their demands were opposed by both major parties. Scotland's faltering economy under the Conservatives in 1951–64 helped to increase support for Labour, which defeated the Conservatives by 43 seats to 23 in 1964 and by 46 seats to 20 in 1966. The Liberals and the SNP both of which supported greater autonomy for Scotland also made gains in these elections, though the SNP failed to secure any parliamentary seats.

In the 1960s the Labour government of Harold Wilson introduced a plan to modernize Scotland's economy and retrain its workforce for new industries. Despite these efforts, there was considerable pessimism about the country's economic prospects until the early 1970s, when oil was discovered in the North Sea. During the early 1980s a worldwide recession coincided with a collapse in oil prices and a series of closures of large industrial plants in Scotland, contributing to an increase in unemployment and further pessimism. In response, the British government created special agencies to attract new investment, notably from American electronics companies, with the result that by the 1990s Scotland had become one of Europe's major electronics manufacturing centres.

Scotland's resource industries farming, fishing, and forestry continued to play an important role in its economy, and tourism increased in importance. Revitalization in Glasgow led to its designation as the European Capital of Culture in 1990, and by the end of the 1990s Scotland's "Silicon Glen" the nickname given to the central part of the country that housed the country's high-tech sector produced nearly one-third of Europe's computers, four-fifths of its workstations, and two-thirds of its automatic teller machines.

Although high-tech plants remained important, confidence in the sector was shaken at the turn of the 21st century by the closure of a number of high-profile plants during the worldwide economic slowdown.

North Sea oil and the rise of Scottish nationalism

In the early 1970s the SNP enjoyed some short-lived electoral success, especially as the flow of North Sea oil increased support for Scottish independence. Campaigning for the October 1974 election on the slogan "It's Scotland's oil!," the SNP managed to mobilize a sense of economic grievance and cultural resentment that cut across the traditional class divisions of Scottish politics. The party won more than 30 percent of the Scottish vote and 11 of the 71 Scottish seats in Parliament.

On March 1, 1979, in an effort to stave off militant nationalism, the Labour government of James Callaghan held a referendum to approve its devolution legislation, which was designed to grant Scotland its own assembly with limited legislative and executive powers. Although favoured by a majority (52.9 percent) of the Scots who voted, the referendum failed to win the approval of the required 40 percent of the electorate. The SNP (along with the Liberals and the Plaid Cymru) then withdrew its support from the Labour government, causing it to lose a vote of confidence, and in the ensuing election the SNP lost 9 of its 11 seats in Parliament.

Despite economic and political problems in the 1980s Scottish cultural confidence grew in most areas of artistic activity. Established Scottish writers such as Alasdair Gray and James Kelman pursued new themes in Scottish literature. They were joined by a new generation of younger writers, notably Irvine Welsh, whose novel Trainspotting (1993) was made into a successful film.

Throughout the 1980s, when the Conservative government in London enjoyed little support in Scotland, support for greater political autonomy increased. In 1989 the introduction in Scotland of the "community charge," a uniform-rate poll tax intended to replace taxation based on property, produced widespread protests against the Conservatives and Prime Minister Margaret Thatcher. (The poll tax was introduced in England and Wales in the following year.) Partly because of the SNP's strong opposition to the poll tax and Labour's lukewarm response, the SNP's support spiked to 21.5 percent of the Scottish vote in 1992 though it won only 3 seats in Parliament, because of the plurality election system; the Labour Party won 49 seats, the Conservatives 11, and the Liberal Democrats 9. Despite Labour's continued popularity in Scotland, the SNP managed to remain a significant presence.

The establishment of a Scottish Parliament

After Labour won a landslide victory in the general elections of May 1997 in which the Conservatives lost all their Scottish seats and the SNP took 6 seats in Parliament the Labour government of Tony Blair called a referendum for establishing a Scottish Parliament with a broad range of powers, including control over the country's education and health systems. Supported by the SNP and the Liberal Democrats but opposed by the Conservatives the referendum passed with more than 74 percent of voters in favour; 64 percent also approved giving the body the power to change tax rates.

Despite opposition from the Conservative Party and the House of Lords, the government adopted a proportional representation system for elections to the new Scottish Parliament, which made it possible for the SNP to extend its influence. At the first elections to the Scottish Parliament in May 1999, Labour won 56 seats, the SNP 35, the Conservatives 18, and the Liberal Democrats 17, while the Greens and the Scottish Socialists each took one seat (an independent candidate captured the remaining seat). Labour and the Liberal Democrats formed a coalition government, with Labour's Donald Dewar assuming the title of first minister.

Dewar considered the "father of devolution" died in 2000 and was replaced by Henry McLeish. McLeish's tenure as first minister was also short-lived, as he was forced to resign the following year because of financial irregularities. Despite being led by three first ministers in the first three years of the Scottish Parliament and severe policy disagreements within the Labour–Liberal Democrat coalition, particularly on education policy, the governing coalition endured, and the Scottish Parliament began to develop into a mature, responsible legislative body, highlighted by its intense but civil debate over war in Iraq in 2003.

In the Scottish Parliament's second election, in May 2003, support for Labour and the SNP dropped (they won 50 and 27 seats, respectively), while the Liberal Democrats and the Conservatives performed at roughly the same level as in 1999. Notably, minor parties increased their seats in the Scottish Parliament significantly, with the Greens winning 7 seats, the Scottish Socialists 6, and independents 4. Still, Labour and the Liberal Democrats continued in coalition. In 2005 the Parliament moved into its permanent building at Holyrood. Devolution permitted Scotland to develop distinctive policies, on such topics as financial support for students and land reform, while in the cultural sphere the establishment of a National Theatre of Scotland filled a gap in the artistic landscape.

In the 2007 elections, the SNP staged a historic upset, winning the most seats (47) in the Scottish Parliament to end some 50 years of Labour Party dominance in Scotland; Labour finished second with 46 seats, and the Conservatives placed third with 17. SNP leader Alex Salmond was subsequently elected first minister of Scotland, becoming the first Nationalist to hold the post. Salmond won a second term in 2011 as the SNP surged to secure a majority in Scotland's Parliament. SNP gains came at the expense of Labour and the Liberal Democrats. With an overall SNP majority, Salmond was able to secure the approval of the Scottish body for a referendum on independence for Scotland.

In 2012 he and British Prime Minister David Cameron signed an agreement to hold that referendum in 2014. Cameron agreed to the wording of the referendum question and to a lowering of the voting age to 16 for the referendum. However, Salmond had to relinquish his demand for a second question that would have given the Scots the option of backing more powers for the Scottish Parliament if a majority of Scots rejected full independence. The referendum, to be held in September 2014, was to pose a single simple question: "Should Scotland be an independent country?" Vigorous campaigns were conducted on both sides of the question.

Opinion polls in 2013 indicated clear sustained opposition to independence by margins ranging between three to two and two to one. Scotland appeared to be polarized between supporters of the SNP, about 4 in 10 Scottish adults, who overwhelmingly backed independence, and the majority of Scots, who both supported the Britain-wide political parties and opposed independence. More than 4.2 million Scots 97 percent of Scotland's residents were registered to vote.

As the day of voting approached, the "yes" side began to gain tremendous momentum, and opinion polling indicated that the outcome was very much in question, though the "no" side held an edge. Former British prime minister Gordon Brown of the Labour Party, a Scot, played a prominent role as an opponent of independence, but he called for debate to be held in the House of Commons on the future of the union in the event that the referendum was defeated. He also outlined a plan that called for codification of the purpose of the United Kingdom akin to the U.S. Declaration of Independence, for recognition of the Scottish Parliament as permanent and indissoluble, and for greater income taxing powers for Scotland.

Only days before the vote, Cameron, Deputy Prime Minister Nick Clegg of the Liberal Party, and Labour Party leader Ed Miliband jointly published in the Scottish newspaper National Record a pledge to increase powers for Scotland's government if the referendum was rejected. When the day of the vote, September 18, arrived, more than 3.6 million Scots (about 85 percent of registered voters) went to the polls and convincingly defeated the referendum, 55 percent voting "no" and 45 percent voting "yes."

In May 2016 the SNP won the election for the Scottish Parliament for the third straight time, though it lost its outright majority, dropping from a total of 69 seats in 2011 to 63 in 2016. Nevertheless. Nicola Sturgeon who had succeeded Salmond as leader of the SNP and first minister in 2014 chose not to form a coalition government, opting instead for minority rule in the belief that election results were still a mandate for her party to continue in power alone. Not only did the results reveal Labour's influence in Scotland to have ebbed even further, falling from 37 seats to 24, but, to add insult to injury, the Conservatives, long largely irrelevant players in Scottish politics, passed Labour to secure 31 seats in Parliament, a gain of 16 seats.

Sturgeon became a vocal opponent of the movement to withdraw the United Kingdom from the European Union, and some 62 percent of Scots who participated in the referendum on "Brexit" on June 23, 2016, voted for Britain to remain within the EU. The majority of those who voted in the United Kingdom as a whole, however, endorsed withdrawal. At the end of March 2017 as Cameron's successor as prime minister, Theresa May, was invoking Article 50 of the Lisbon Treaty and triggering the start of negotiations with the EU on separation Sturgeon sought and won approval from the Scottish Parliament to formally request that the British government grant Scotland the powers necessary to hold a new referendum on independence, to be conducted before spring 2019. In the June 2017 snap election called by May, however, Scottish voters appeared to rebuke Sturgeon's call for a new referendum as the SNP's representation in the British Parliament fell from 56 seats to 35.

www.ingramcontent.com/pod-product-compliance
Lightning Source LLC
Chambersburg PA
CBHW021100080526
44587CB00010B/320